# Make Break Remix: The Rise of K-style

D1453313

# 메이크 MAKE BREAK브레이크 리REMIX

# THE RISE OF K-STYLE

**Fiona Bae**
Photographs by less_TAEKYUN KIM

# Contents

# Foreword

## Na Kim

Na Kim is a graphic designer based in Berlin and Seoul. As an artist, she has taken part in numerous exhibitions at major art museums and galleries such as the MMCA, Seoul, the Victoria and Albert Museum, London, and MoMA, New York, among others. Boldly yet naturally crossing the boundary between design and art, she has provided young Korean creators with a new role model. Kim has been a curator for Fikra Graphic Design Biennial, Chaumont Graphic Design Festival and Seoul International Typography Biennale. She led space design for the V&A's 2022 exhibition 'Hallyu! The Korean Wave'.

When I arrived in the Netherlands to study in 2006, many people commented that my design didn't look Asian. This made me wonder what Asian style was; back then, people seemed to associate it with brushstrokes and certain colour schemes. Having since worked in the Netherlands and Berlin, I have often found myself in the position of having to introduce the cultural scene of Korea or Seoul to the outer world. Witnessing the rapid rise of K-style, I also became personally curious about how this global phenomenon was born and evolved. I started to ask deeper questions about its social context. In 2022, my role as a creative lead for the design of an exhibition of Korean pop culture in London enabled me to further delve into what 'K-ness' means from diverse perspectives, and how Korean culture became so influential globally. I tried to figure out the word and themes, to illustrate what's happening in Korean culture. So when I was approached to write the foreword for *Make Break Remix: The Rise of K-style*, I was instantly curious about the choice of the term by its author, Fiona Bae. I asked her what she meant by 'K-style'. She explained that she had come to realize that it went beyond fashion or style; it is an attitude among brave and bold young Koreans who are creating something of their own.

I certainly felt that attitude while working in Korea before I returned to Europe in 2019. Among designers, the younger generation started to just go and do things, without getting hung up on going abroad to study at famous schools like we had. While designing an album cover for Hyukoh, a widely popular indie musician, I found it stimulating when he admitted that he would never be as solid as Shin Jung-hyeon, a legendary Korean godfather of rock. He said that he knows he can never become a big mountain, so he's going to make a small bonfire to celebrate in the mountain instead. Young people in Korea are devouring whatever they find cool and creating whatever they can.

In Korea, favouritism based on schools and regions used to prevail. But from music, to fashion, to literature, young people across sectors who have gathered around the same zeitgeist and vision have created much stronger bonds and a sense of solidarity. Those pursuing what they are passionate about, regardless of their background and which area they came from, have formed strong groups, with a sort of amateurism that has granted them greater flexibility in their thinking. Flexibility and adaptability are big strengths in Korean culture. The availability of communications tools and social media platforms has enabled these groups to activate and spread what they are creating.

People want to understand the social context of the Korean Wave and K-style, and this book addresses it brilliantly through the author's considered introduction and intimate interviews with pioneering artists and creative directors who are actively shaping K-style across different sectors.

I was glad to recognize so many friends and people I admire among the interviewees and people who collaborated on the book. The author has managed to capture the spirit of K-style, producing a seamless flow through the rich content of the interviewees' texts and eye-catching imagery. The book's photographer, less_TAEKYUN KIM, offers a new, refreshing take on Korean youths and the streets of Seoul.

As Bae writes in her introduction, suppression and a social obsession with out-performing happened to bring out the explosion of energy that is 'K'. Korea is full of ironies and contradictions. My parents always reminded me that a cornered stone meets the mason's chisel. People are afraid to stand out, but you cannot be too similar either; you need to be slightly better than the rest.

As I continued researching, I also began to think about how Hallyu goes beyond national boundaries. As seen in K-pop fandoms, it's also a movement of youth beyond Korea. Young people are constantly adding new branches into what was there. Like a life being lived, K-style is hybrid and constantly evolving. While K-pop and K-drama have dominated the scene, I believe that K-style will continue to reveal itself in more diverse forms and areas, including the design scene.

Efforts like this book will provide momentum for international audiences to pay more attention to the future evolution of K-style, which I believe will continue to flourish. K-style is changing as I write, ever in flux.

# Introduction

As a Korean, the rise of Korean culture in music, drama and fashion initially made me proud but left me a bit perplexed. Growing up in a small country shaped by a heady mix of cultural influences from China and Japan, under the heavy influence of the US, and with the constant existential threat posed by North Korea, we were almost forced to be proud to mask our insecurity. As a result, I became very weary of any nationalistic propaganda. When the Korean press boasted of foreign newspapers' high praise for anything Korean, I would look up the original articles and inevitably find that it had been widely exaggerated. No longer. Having witnessed the rich, authentic creativity of young Koreans, I don't feel the need to verify what I can see with my own eyes. Having worked alongside great talent and seen increasing success while promoting Korean designers, architects and artists during many years in international communications, I became passionate about making a book that would illustrate the driving forces and future direction of K–style. This book doesn't aim to define K–style. Instead, we are offering a snapshot of Korea — one of the most influential style hubs on the planet — in evolution.

The ingredients for K–style's success have long been present: hard–working people with a huge appetite for learning based in the values of Confucianism, a love for singing and dancing together, and an adaptability and practicality that have roots in Shamanism, and a hyper–competitiveness and yearning for international recognition resulting from a rapidly developing society. Combined with the context of technology, which broadened Koreans' tastes and imagination, and a corresponding questioning of Western–centric values, and BOOM! K–style exploded.

Korea has gone through a remarkable transformation over the last few decades. Emerging from the ruins of the Japanese occupation and the Korean War, South Korea remained among the poorest countries in the world into the 1960s. Democracy only started in 1988, the year that Seoul hosted the Olympic Games after years of dictatorships and military government. Until then, we had not been allowed to travel overseas for leisure, because the government worried that North Koreans would 'turn' us. To support and boost exports, the practice of copying products from Japan or Western countries, from lamps and radios to televisions, was widely accepted. Being a small country reliant on stronger countries exacerbated Korea's insecurity and longing for external recognition, and rapid economic development made Korean society extremely competitive, materialistic and status–driven. Riven by economic and political turmoil, people were afraid to stand out, and a herd mentality dominated. Young women used to wear the same makeup, and young guys had the same haircut. Even until a few years ago, cars in Seoul were predominantly black, white and silver.

Young Koreans might look more individualistic now, but even most fashion-conscious hipsters will demonstrate relatively strong communal bonding in their fashion choices. The path to success felt clearly but narrowly defined. But such suppression also brought about the rebellious spirit that suffuses K-style.

As a small country with passionate and industrious people, Korea progressed from exporting cars and phones to exporting culture, as our wealth developed and tastes became more discerning. Slowly, the Korean government, which had traditionally focused resources on local mega-corporations called Chaebol as a quick fix for a poor economy, began to increase support for the cultural scene, recognizing its potential as another successful export. For a small country, independence means so much, and culture is seen as the best way of building a new international presence; the government is now thrilled to ride the popularity of K-style by claiming a critical role in its development. This has helped in its own way, but contrary to recurrent narratives in the West, I believe the success of K-style was driven foremost by individual creators. Korean pop culture first became big across Asia by digesting and adapting Western stories and sounds for regional audiences. We went on to reinterpret and remix Western and Asian styles in pop music and drama. K-pop and K-drama deliver universal stories with an attitude that appeals to wider audiences disenchanted by the cultural dominance of the West.

Ultimately, K-style is a bold and brave attitude pioneered by young Koreans, remixing everything they find to be cool with zero inhibition. Breaking out of traditionally oppressive social constraints, K-style celebrates newfound confidence, pride and independence. It has resonated across continents with those who want to rebel against the old order and make something of their own. In a world where the boundaries between originality and copying are increasingly blurry, the mix created by K-style can lead to a 'new authenticity'. The title of this book, *Make Break Remix*, celebrates this creative process. Among younger generations, hypersensitive consumers of digital media who immediately see through fakery, this genuine, raw approach is vital to K-style's success.

K-style is open to layers of interpretation, as seen through the eclectic mix of influential, creative people featured in these pages. Interviews with trailblazers across different aspects of K-style are interspersed with five distinct photo essays: interviewee portraits, K-fashion among Seoul's youth, landscapes and cityscapes, street style and our interviewees' creative environments. And what bigger influence than the city and people of Seoul itself? The colours of this vast, vibrant city have been painted in words and photographs. Respected for his deep understanding of Seoul youth culture and his frequent work for publications including *GQ* and *Vogue*, photographer less_TAEKYUN KIM shows the atypical, intimate side of the city with his raw, low-key pictures, dotted with the city's stylish and daring youth and our interviewees.

Seoul is highly dense and chaotic, with buildings tumbling over each other. You take a subway for fifteen minutes and walk out into another bustling centre. But it's easy to embrace this chaos once you realize how aptly it reflects the energy of the city. Some mayors have been obsessed with developing a landmark in Seoul, but its first City Architect, Seung H. Sang, who shifted Seoul's direction from urban growth to regeneration, reminded us that the four mountains surrounding the city are its best landmark. As I write this book, relatively underdeveloped neighbourhoods are emerging as next-generation hotspots. Dynamic architecture and hyper-aesthetic, trendy shops are juxtaposed with big swathes of the old grey city.

Seoul changes so fast. Some people argue that the cultural transformations that happened in places like Brooklyn and Shoreditch over ten years happened in Seoul in a single year. Trends come here to flourish and die. Koreans get excited very fast, but bored even faster. Our strong conformist streak has led to a million people striving to achieve the same look, and communal bonding among peers is still very visible here. Speed and competition are deeply woven into Korean society. You cannot afford to fall behind on trends. It has astounding energy, but it can be exhausting for those at the cutting edge.

Just like Seoul, what makes K-style fascinating is its complex mix and contrast of the old and the new, Western and Eastern, high- and low-brow. Through its interviews and photos, *Make Break Remix* offers a snapshot of the shapeshifting, trendsetting worlds of K-style. Our trailblazing interviewees are not the typical K-pop idols or K-drama actors, whose individual creativity is often curbed in order to conform to business-driven norms and formulas. Many of the people in this book are instead leaders in subculture scenes. These are the people looked up to by the K-pop stars, insiders who are creating the trends before anyone even starts taking notice.

We will hear about the making of K-pop from those responsible for propelling it into the global spotlight, including choreographer Lia Kim, whose 1MILLION Dance Studio has twenty-five million YouTube subscribers, and Youngjin Kim, stylist for K-pop group NCT, who pulls off a balancing act: breaking the mould of typical K-pop styling while keeping his boyband's fans happy. The music industry's intriguing underside is explored by Lim

Kim, the K-pop idol turned independent musician who helped break away from the idea of female submission, and Hwang Soyoon, a popular young Korean rock star and leader of the band Sae So Neon, adored by musicians including Ryuichi Sakamoto. DPR REM, founder and creative director of music collective DPR, manifests a compelling alternative to the K-pop factory. Kyuhee Baik, head of Stüssy Korea and strategy director for celebrated Seoul-based brand Hyein Seo, Serian Heu, visual director at BTS's label Hybe and former digital director at *Vogue* Korea, and Jieun Seo and Jiyoon Jung, founders of street fashion brand Mischief, each discuss how subcultures and mainstream fashion scenes interact in Seoul, and how strong camaraderie makes their foreign friends envious of them living in Seoul. Xu Meen, the first Asian male model to appear on the cover of the *New York Times*'s *T Magazine*, talks about how his inspiration is himself. Designer Kwangho Lee and interior designer Teo Yang shed light on the increasingly influential design side of K-style and their ongoing quests for identity, and Mingoo Kang, a pioneer of new Korean dining, tells of his passion for Korean fried chicken (KFC, as he calls it) and the evolving food scenes of Seoul.

We talk about what brought the current K-style boom about, including Korea's digital transformation and newfound cultural confidence. You'll find refreshingly different views on the individualism nurtured by social media — and not everyone loves Seoul. BAJOWOO of Korean label %99IS-, who has a cult following among LA musicians, has more hate than love for his native city, which told him time after time, 'you can't do it'. Our interviewees demonstrate resilience and resistance in this rapidly changing world, challenging norms from beauty standards to gender stereotypes. In a country where tattooing is criminalized, tattoo artist Doy has created a new style of delicate fine-line tattoos to attract a new breed of customer. Now, his tattoo studio is a must-stop for Hollywood stars visiting Seoul, such as Lily Collins and Brad Pitt. Korean society imposes strong constraints on any kind of diversity, so how refreshing that not only the LGBTQ+ community but also straight women admire drag artist Nana Youngrong Kim for standing out.

In the 'Commentators' section, Danny Chung, A&R and songwriter for stars such as Blackpink, offers compelling observations on the evolution of K-pop. Elaine YJ Lee, who writes for *i-D* and *Hypebeast*, shares her inside story of digital fashion media and K-beauty, while Jason Schlabach adds an animating portrait of the Seoul streets from his days as brand director at Seoul's iconoclastic RYSE Hotel. The Korean Fashion Directory, compiled and photographed by renowned fashion editor Sukwoo Hong (a.k.a. Your Boyhood), tells the intimate stories of the making of four noteworthy Seoul-based labels: PAF, The Museum Visitor, After Pray and DOCUMENT.

Korea is going through a fragile transition. People have begun to realize that personal assessment of our choices can be more important than external validation. While breaking the mould, young Koreans are in a deep search for their identity. The geopolitical threats and competitiveness of the past remain, but the playing field has changed in order for young creators to flourish. Korea used to feel too small for fiercely driven people. But social media and new technology have enabled young Koreans to turn their aspirations into a global reality. There is an explosive energy and solidarity among young creatives now. Architects, photographers and musicians are gathering to ride a big wave they have been waiting for together. That's what made it possible for this book to be born. My interviewees are testament that with passion and a sustained meditation on creating something of one's own, K-style will continue to reveal itself in strong, diverse forms.

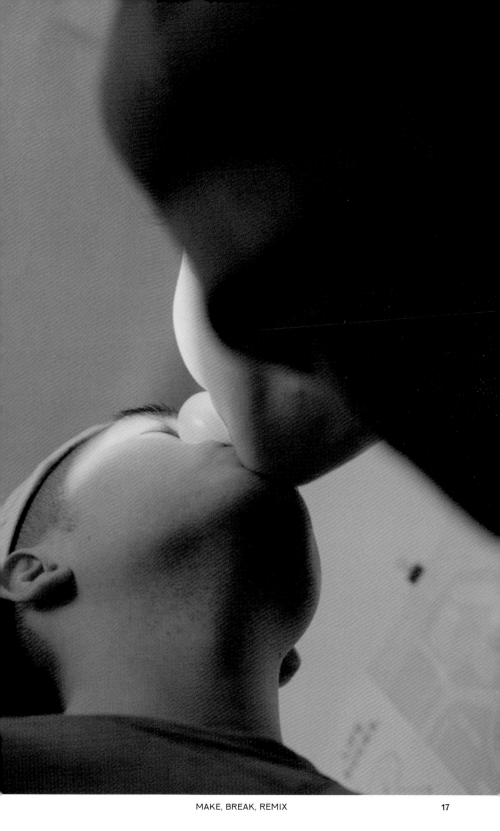

MAKE, BREAK, REMIX

MAKE, BREAK, REMIX

MAKE, BREAK, REMIX

MAKE, BREAK, REMIX

# 나리와 Kim김

**Choreographer, artist, founder of 1MILLION Dance Studio**

## On her style and influences

When I started dancing, I was inspired by the older generation of
dancers in Los Angeles who originated Popping, my speciality. The
dance culture is rooted in LA, so it continued to influence me after
I started choreographing. I like watching films and music videos, in
particular ones with the feel of a drama rather than videos that are
perfectly set. I want to create a cinematographic look and deliver
a story through my dance.

 I don't have much desire for everyday clothes. I wear all black
training clothes, whatever's easy to move in. I approach fashion
through my artistic work. I envision the concept of my work and dress
myself to match the big idea I have. I delve into my identity when I'm
interviewed by the press. I seem to be sandwiched in the middle of
lots of roles: an artist, dance trainer, CEO and fashionista. I just try
to choose a style that feels like me and is comfortable. Some witty
fan posted on social media, 'Lia Kim.... Hold my weird but unique
long sleeve collection'. Perhaps that's my style signifier.

 When I develop choreography, I try to remove my own
style entirely and focus on the specific character and strength of
the artist. I imagine I'm Sunmi when I work with her. Instead of
building a grand composition with impressive dance moves, I ask,
'what facial expression or movement does Sunmi need to look most
charming when she sings this line?' Unique choreography stems from
expressions, characters and attitudes, rather than specific movements.
Once I've done the artist's steps, I fill the stage with backup dancers
like arranging a bouquet. I welcome ideas from the artist and labels
to develop the direction. Then once I start, I don't let them interfere.
I don't share it until I send a completed demo tape. Even excellent
choreography never looks that cool when it's shown in a rough form.

리아킴

## On living rurally and working in Seoul

We moved our studio to Seongsu-dong, a vibrant neighbourhood full of various cultures, because of its trendy atmosphere and mix of young and old people. Seoul is like that. I moved to a rural town in Yangpyeong to be away from the fast-moving life. It's perfect for watering flowers and walking a dog. Korea still tends to be swept away by trends. I want to show that artists who are not 'trendy' can be a good influence.

I am a K-pop choreographer who needs to connect with the mainstream, and an artist who expresses my own feelings as if I don't care about the public's reaction. In the past, I felt obliged to choose between these, but doing both is more fun and challenging.

## On the rise of K-style

The speed of content production and consumption is extremely fast here. Two weeks' promotion on air is all that musicians get after working so hard on releasing a new album. People quickly forget and want new content, which can feel empty. I wonder whether it is worthwhile to put in so much effort to create something outstanding. But on the other hand, we've been super well trained to extract the best quality content fastest.

People say, '1MILLION seems to lead K-style dance', but in fact, we are just listening to music and expressing it. Perhaps we were able to absorb everything and produce something because we never tried to establish our own style. That might be K-style.

## On training K-pop artists, and the popularity of 1MILLION Studio

When uploading videos of our dance classes for 1MILLION Studio, I feel the key is to keep it as real as possible so that people feel they're with us. While other dance studios try for a perfectly polished look, we go for raw. We don't remove the water bottles and clothes students leave on the dance floor when we shoot. We include the reaction of students craning their necks to watch and cheering for other students while waiting for their class.

As a K-pop artist trainer, my role is to shape raw talent into stars. Trainees find dance training most difficult, so labels put dance teachers in charge of becoming mentors and disciplining trainees. I also handle the overall expression and attitude of artists, so that they perform perfectly when they debut.

Trainees follow strict rules, with little freedom or chance to express their individuality for years. They are hard-working and respect orders, which helps them learn difficult dance moves quickly. Korea established a big entertainment system to nurture talent. Kids are able to receive training from experts for years, and this sort of hardcore training builds teamwork.

## On the changing style and status of K-pop

In the early days, my work was often rejected for being too strong and artsy. Experience taught me that labels focusing on the cuteness and sex appeal of artists didn't fit me, so I went to work with companies that were more invested in clear concepts and storytelling. I feel that K-pop is still centred around certain looks. Less than ten per cent of artists have distinctive positioning. But lately I feel that the choreography allows for bolder expressions. Increasingly, I'm able to get involved in the early concept-development stage. Some labels say, 'Tell us what you envision, and we will create the music'. They seek my advice on artists' styling and develop music videos based on my choreography.

K-pop used to have a longing to emulate American style and music. Because of its influence and commercial success, many choreographers in LA have developed a keen interest in working with Korean labels. I get more and more calls from LA asking to collaborate. Their attitude has clearly changed. Now in LA, if you work with K-pop artists, you are considered to be the best.

## On what's next

I like storytelling, and I'm interested in unknown worlds. How dancers and choreography look when viewed in videos rather than on stage matters more now. It should look beautiful in small images and angles like on TikTok, so I am adapting to a new style. The era of home training for dance through VR is coming, so I am figuring out how I can play a role there.

1milliondance.com
instagram @liakimhappy

# You 김영진 Kim

Stylist for K-pop musicians such as boyband NCT

## On his style and influences

I love music. I get inspiration from film and TV series rather than high fashion. I love going to aquariums and learning colouring from fish. I also like going to buy flowers. I'm crazy about vintage or classic furniture and design.

While I don't like styling others in only black, I don't wear much colour. When I do, I go for something really vivid, but I still match it with black trousers. I own so much black clothing. I only wear black socks. I feel uneasy if I don't have something black on. I must have fifty pairs of black trousers at least. I love classic items.

When I am preparing for important work, I push myself more, to absorb as much as possible. I'll take a longer shower or stay longer in the bathroom to wait for ideas to pop up. I used to jot things down on my hand. I would write ideas for one of my musicians' posters on my hands. It would spread to cover my palm, wrist and forearm.

I like going through old books for inspiration. With trends changing so fast, there is a limit to how many new things can come out. I read about old classic fashion and I catch what's coming next, then I mix and match them. NCT is a future-orientated group, and I need to conceive a clear concept beyond fashion. I sometimes get cues from watching Japanese animations from my teen days.

## On living and working in Seoul

Seoul stresses me out and pushes me to work without sleep, but I fall back in love when I drive across the river in the morning.

Koreans excel at absorbing new trends, they do it the best in Asia, although Korea has been criticized for copying. Most men in

Seoul care about fashion and look stylish. They'll open their wallets for clothes.

## On styling for K-pop

K-pop styling has a unique feature: while stylists in other countries tend to deal with one musician, we have to fill the stage with between seven and nine idols.

Balancing what I want with what idols' fans fancy is always challenging. The entertainment labels care about fans' reactions because they want to sell more music. Many fans want idols to dress like their boyfriends. I like putting boots on NCT, but fans want sneakers. I do take the fans' sides sometimes. I dress NCT like princes for awards ceremonies. Foreign fans often welcome daring attempts more, but I don't consciously think about who to appeal to. I try to strike a balance.

For NCT, who I've worked with for over three years, I take the member who wasn't interested in fashion at first out shopping and to tattoo studios. I recommend films and designer chairs. I feel proud watching the members' tastes become polished. I struggle when I work on commercials that don't require genuine styling. Cosmetics and food commercials also need the models to wear something. I have to follow clients' direction to make money.

Several years ago, I wouldn't take K-pop work because it felt like no fun. The labels requested safe and typical styling. When SM Entertainment asked me to work with NCT, they surprised me by saying I could do whatever I wanted. They chose me to elevate the fashion in their group. These days, they even offer me a bigger budget on outfits, because they understand the importance of visuals.

김영진

## On the challenges of music videos

We often work to crazy deadlines with last-minute changes. A final song will keep changing, or a music video director will refuse the visuals two days before the shoot.

I focus on the role of each member in a particular song: 'I need to make him shine when he's doing a special move'. I reflect on each of their physiques. The idol needs to demonstrate their best feature within the three minutes of the music video. If the outfit doesn't suit them or they don't feel secure in it, it can impact their confidence. I try to talk it up.

Outfits must make the band stand out, but the boys should also be able to dance. Most trousers are no good because they don't stretch enough. Trousers with a wide leg won't underline a clean-cut dance move. So we often produce garments ourselves. I can then switch custom-made clothing among the team members on set to find a better match.

Seoul offers great support for this, from raw materials to skilled pattern-makers to seamstresses. There are several studios that specialize in K-pop, but few can produce unique clothes with new techniques. I cannot afford for imperfect costumes to turn up on the set of a music video, so I work with only one studio I've built trust with. Sometimes they work for two or three nights to produce outfits for nine members.

I successfully worked with designer Kanghyuk to create costumes for NCT once. But often instead of two or three months, I get two weeks to complete costumes, which makes it nearly impossible to work with talented designers.

## On the rise of K-style

Mandatory military service had a big impact on the male beauty industry's growth in Korea. Guys dived into *GQ* and *Esquire* because there wasn't much else to do. They learned about grooming and bought beauty products as an entry point (to fashion) before buying clothes.

K-pop has influenced people to follow idols' style. It fixates on strong visuals, but the music deserves more attention. With a focus on music, I hope K-pop will remain admired instead of being a fad. Like LPs from decades ago that I collect, I want K-pop to stay around.

I see my role as ensuring people don't get tired of K-pop. I don't consciously try to express something Korean, but I think it comes out naturally.

youngjinkim.com
instagram @kimvenchy

# DPR IAN REM

Founder and creative director of DPR music collective

## On his inspiration and style

My father is my inspiration in terms of how I work. He was in the footwear business in the US and Korea for over thirty-five years. He believed in what he did and was deeply rooted in it. Similarly, I look up to creative directors who are not only deeply invested in their work, but also multifaceted and in tune with many sectors.

I like to think I have a reserved sense of style, but always with something that is eye-catching. I was born and raised in New York and moved to Korea in my early twenties. At first, I seemed very 'New York', but the more time I spent here, the more I dived into the Korean culture. It's not style. It's more persona. The whole persona of New York can be rough, cold and very direct. In Korea, there are times when it works, but there are times you can't be too New York. Learning that ability to know 'In this situation, I'd better be this way' was the key.

I like the idea of having a sense of mystery, which I think is heavily reflected in the style I created for DPR. Especially in these times where social media is constantly utilized and artists or labels tend to show everything about themselves, we believe our art should speak for itself. 'If you like what we do, welcome aboard'. The element of surprise engages with our fans. And that leads to more personal, long-term support. You know who really supports you. We feel our fans now know how we operate.

## On the birth of DPR

I met DPR IAN when I first came to Korea in 2014. We kind of started DPR from that point on, just doing what we liked, whether musically or visually.

I think we both felt like Korea was still premature with regards to entertainment and what was possible. We saw lots of problems come from trying to connect business with creative. 'Artist vs management', so to speak. That said, I think that's what really drove us. The fact that you could connect the two and make great things happen. And what better than to do it ourselves — especially among friends!

Basically, we believe in a very DIY culture. Unlike big entertainment labels, which work as a huge system or chain of command, we have a free-flowing style. Whatever we think is cool, we just go for it. We have a very democratic approach, in that almost all decisions are made through team votes, and that is very rare in this entertainment scene. As a team, we definitely come together and

디피알 렘

move as one when we execute something. We tend to go very quiet when we work, because we need control and focus to make our final product as precise as possible. And we love the reaction from our fans, which is a huge driver. It's like planning a surprise birthday party for a close friend.

## On living and working in Seoul

I think it's amazing. As a still-young, growing economy, Korea offers great opportunities and has so much room to grow. Like I've stated before, I'm an American. However, I'm also proud to be a Korean. I came to the country that my parents are from to draw inspiration from it, and now I'm trying to push what I reinterpret in Korea globally. At DPR, we all have some sort of Korean heritage but come from diverse backgrounds, such as the US, Australia, Guam — and I think this is what led to our movement being so different and unique. We have so many different perspectives that, when we come together on a project, it always feels somehow new to everyone. We took Korea's biggest industry, the entertainment business, into our own hands, and are now putting it back out to the world through our collective lens.

## On being independent and self-sustainable

We focused on what we were good at and set up our own video production team in DPR. In the beginning we shot random videos and posted them on social media. Through word of mouth, entertainment companies started hitting us up, and that is how we began shooting music videos for third-party artists. We used all these opportunities to save up and invest in our own production — musically — and that's what led to our first 'artist', DPR LIVE, and his debut EP, *Coming To You Live*.

We felt we were selling ourselves short a bit when we were shooting for others, so we stopped completely. We now only shoot DPR-related stuff, because we don't want anybody to tell us what to do or touch our vision. At other big labels, the thought process is very different. There are too many people who need to approve, too many restrictions. It's like at some point it just kills the passion and becomes a nuisance.

In order to be self-sustainable, we felt that we needed to grow through our own social channels and our own community. There was no fluff. We didn't get here through any buzz from outside, like TV or radio shows. Instead, we get support straight from our fans.

We're not against appearing on TV, we just really enjoy the system we have in place right now, as we can control what gets put out and how it gets put out. With broadcasts or whatnot, I think you lose that freedom. On a side note, it's also a testament to ourselves that we can still succeed solely relying on each other's work ethic and passion. That's what a team really means and that's the message we want the general public to take note of. All you need is a solid team and a collective passion for something. Then the world is yours for the taking.

## On DPR clothing

We'd got a lot of requests and fans asking us what we wear, and naturally we just thought 'why not make our own stuff'. All of our clothes start with a custom template — compiling as much as we can as a team to put out whatever we collectively think is cool. We don't necessarily stick to a timeline — we do it more as a passion project. We just recently did a collection with the IISE brand, and that really stemmed from our relationship. Since we were already close, we thought it would be a great idea to just work on something together and have it offer something new for not only each other, but for the public. The process happened very organically. I remember we had a big workshop where the IISE team came over to our studio, and they

디피알 렘

had everyone sit down and just draw any type of inspiration/thought/ memory they had, given certain topics or themes. From these random drawings, they compiled possible design concepts, and we just went with whatever we collectively liked. And that's how the collection 'DPR DREAMS CURATED BY IISE' came about.

## On the rise of K-style

Korea has become a content powerhouse. If something is cool, it goes viral instantly. You have the world as your audience. This current age is so virtual, so fast, so accessible. On the other hand, personally, I think as more time goes by and we're more connected digitally, it's also really important to have that personal time to still be a bit analogue — enjoy the real world, so to speak.

In the entertainment world, lots of young kids start working a lot earlier. When I started at twenty-four, twenty-five, I thought I was very young, but I see younger kids producing now. With technology, young people have become in a sense a bit more entrepreneurial. You don't need to get a record deal any more, you can just post on social media, make a song, and with the right buzz, you'll be recognized.

K-style is still evolving. There are still so many layers to peel back. K-pop is a great introduction to Korean culture, but there is so much more that has yet to be discovered. We believe we can bring more diversity to the Korean music scene. Our goal is to add different and newer flavours through the exchange of cultures, our members' personal experiences and backgrounds.

## On DPR's goals

Our biggest goal is to leave a legacy — to be remembered as a team that really pushed boundaries and made people feel something deeper than surface-level entertainment. Also, to show people that anything you dream of really is possible — I came to Korea not knowing how to speak the language or understanding the culture, let alone knowing how to distribute music or operate an entertainment label. Nonetheless, now that I look back at the past five years, having come this far, it really goes to show that you can make your wildest imaginations a reality — you just need an unwavering conviction in your goals and to surround yourself with the right people.

dreamperfectregime.com
instagram @dprrem

# 'K-style mixes everything cool with urgency. It commands immediate attention.'

— Marc Cansier, founding partner of Marc & Chantal

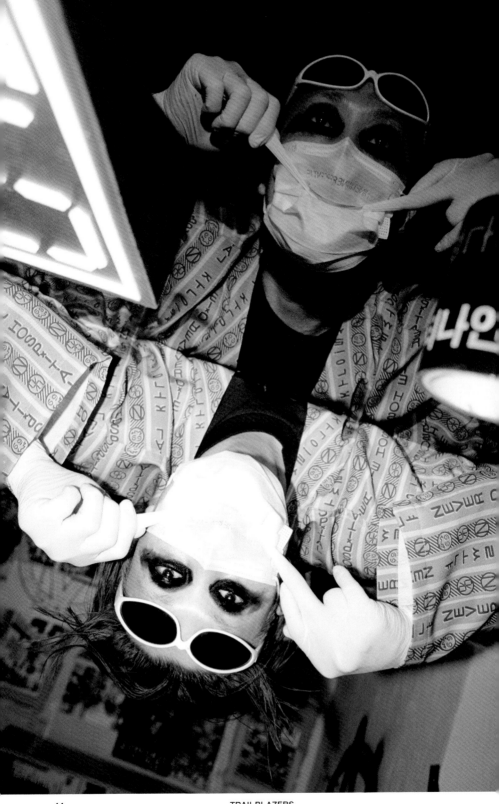

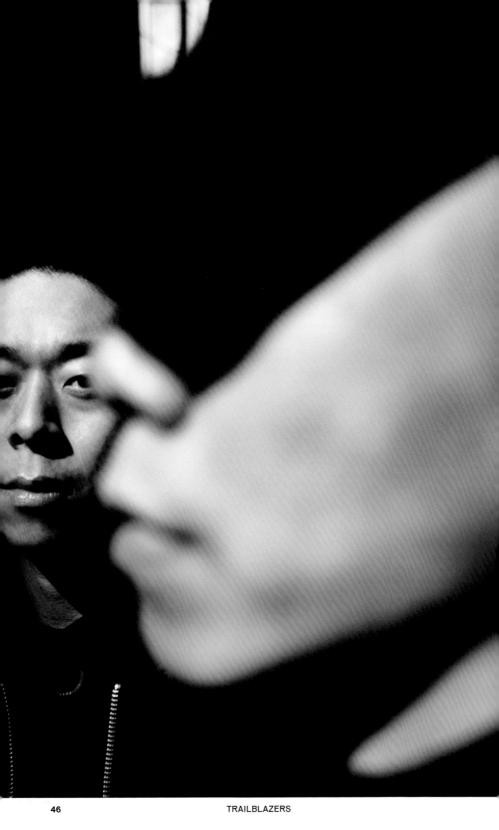

TRAILBLAZERS

TRAILBLAZERS

TRAILBLAZERS

TRAILBLAZERS

TRAILBLAZERS

TRAILBLAZERS

TRAILBLAZERS

TRAILBLAZERS

TRAILBLAZERS

Leading Korean fashion model

## On his style and influences

My inspiration for my style is myself. I was probably picked for this book because people felt strongly when they saw me and couldn't think of someone else. I prefer to be a 'Xu Meen' who has an influence on someone, rather than a 'Xu Meen' formed by someone else's influence.

Rather than simply expressing 'Xu Meen' in one way, I'm seen through the many diverse roles given to me. There may be complex factors in the formation of my character. It's about the culture of the times I live in, the thoughts I had at that time.... I don't even know what exactly it is. But it is difficult to say those elements are directly projected into my style; everything seems to be expressed in my style after the filter 'Xu Meen' is applied.

In my work, I try to understand how things should be done in advance, before starting a photoshoot. Even on set, I have constant conversations with the designers and the creative director about what they want to capture.

I think the highest level of confidence in yourself is also critical. You have to be convinced that you are the best in your area. Only then, if you do something, will people accept that you're the best. If you don't have confidence in yourself, it doesn't make sense to expect it to come out naturally in a fashion show or a photoshoot. What feels awkward will obviously show.

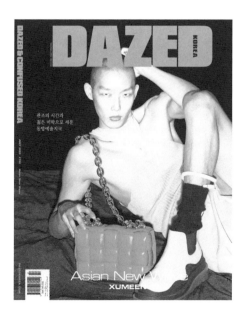

김수민

## On what he enjoys about modelling

Everything I experience as a model is valuable, beyond what I can describe in words. Seeing, hearing and feeling a wide range of new cultures, people, languages and values while travelling to and from numerous cities in different countries is a great joy for me and makes me grow even further.

At fashion shows, the liveliness you get from the runway drives people crazy. A show typically lasts for between ten and twenty minutes. It is live, and within that time the attention and concentration from all over the world, the lighting, sounds of cameras and everyone pouring out praise take my adrenaline above its peak.

Photographers will wait outside the show to take the models' photos. They'll call out my name, ask me to look at their cameras. I move to the next fashion show, and everything repeats. During fashion weeks, I walk several shows a day. It's hard to describe.

Photoshoots or commercial shoots have a different attraction. It takes real teamwork to create the best results by collaborating with leading brands and teams. Compared to fashion shows, commercials create exposure anytime and anywhere, to people who are not interested in fashion or do not know about fashion.

The charms of each runway and photo set are different, and the energy I gain from them makes me feel like the person called 'Xu Meen' again.

## On becoming a successful model

How many people around you are models? Not an Instagrammer, Tik-Toker, blogger, but a model. I think the job is at least ninety-nine per cent innate. Persona, appearance, height, proportions and talent all have to match. Then, that last one per cent doesn't have a definite answer.

Of course, a job as a model can include flair and talent. However, whether it's lucky or not, first of all, you should be able to express enough of your charms with just your appearance. When you walk a runway or appear in a commercial you embody a fantasy. That is what people's decision will be based on.

## On life in Seoul

I spend a lot of time abroad, so returning to Korea after a long period of time is a vacation I commit to. I meet with Korean friends that I haven't seen for a long time. Having this time makes me not forget my identity as a Korean.

## On the rise of K-style

As a model, I represent various brands, but I am not directly involved in design or styling, so I am not a person who creates K-style. It's difficult to give a clear answer on what K-style is.

Nevertheless, I think you could say that what's special in K-style is 'possibility'. Fashion basically changes with the seasons – not drastically from year to year, but it does always change. Korea is a trend-conscious country, and people like to do things quickly. I think that the understanding and fast flow of fashion in Korea is like the basic nature of fashion. Since the fundamental character of Korea itself contains some of the features of fashion, I look forward to the future of fashion in Korea.

instagram @xumeen

김수민

# Seria 허세란 Heu

Visual Director at Hybe and former Digital Director at *Vogue* Korea

## On her style and influences

I change every season, and I am influenced by designers, musicians and people I shoot photos for. The actress Jeon Do-yeon impressed me when we shot her wearing Off White for *Vogue*. I found it cool for a forty-eight-year-old actress not to be afraid of trying something radically new.

I like many different styles. I style my look depending on my daily mood. I enjoy clothes by emerging designers, including Koreans. Colour and pattern grab my attention. I like mixing high and street fashion. I enjoy a lovely princess look with a baseball cap.

## On her work identity

I always try to go beyond a typical K-pop style by introducing unusual brands. I try to instil an open mind among idols in both a fashion and cultural sense, to appeal to a wider audience. Directing visuals for ENHYPEN at Hybe feels like being the coach of a sports team. New attempts will often be rejected by members of the group. They won't wear a chosen custom piece unless they are fully convinced, so we constantly discuss, which helps me understand them better and get inspired, which is refreshing. Each show and photoshoot feels like a challenging match. I try to make each member develop their distinctive identity while they work in unison on stage. For research, I like looking at books or the websites of photographers or designers. I find Instagram confusing, because it's full of selected images without a proper storyline.

허세련

## On living and working in Seoul

I sometimes wish I lived abroad somewhere like London, to become more creative. Connections like your school and hometown matter too much in mainstream Seoul fashion scenes. The focus on job history and titles more than on capability depresses me. Fortunately, things are changing.

My favourite foreign fashion brands are broadly not available in Korea. Even when they are, the shops stocking them are too stuffy and suffocating. But it's so thrilling to be at the centre of K-pop, which influences global fashion scenes.

## On the rise of K-style

In the past, people needed to really dig in to understand trends. Now anyone can absorb global fashion instantly. While it is almost scary for someone who worked in print magazines, I realize it also helps in spreading K-fashion faster. K-pop represents Asia and brings attention to Korean fashion.

## On trends in Korea

Koreans consume trends too quickly, and eating too fast causes stomach ache. Without clear standards and our own interpretation, we accept it unconditionally. I'm short, but I have bought many clothes that only suit tall women.

To be considered fashionable, once others follow what you had picked, you quickly drop it. Trends come and die super-fast here. But having an international reputation for being unbelievably trendy helps the fashion industry to develop fast and nurture talented designers.

Fashion people love what's rare, because you want to be considered different. Young brands use this knowledge. One local brand, Dada, made a culture of consumers lining up for their limited edition. Peer bonding still prevails. If you go to a cool store in Hongdae, you'll see hipsters with the same style.

## On interactions between subculture and mainstream fashion

Anything cool starts in subculture first and moves to mass culture. Subculture looks down on mass culture and instantly discontinues something when it is picked up in the mainstream. Kanghyuk and Hyein Seo rejected offers to be interviewed for *Vogue* as notable Korean brands. They didn't want to be overexposed in mass media and become too popular.

An intriguing contrast exists between mainstream and subculture fashion scenes. My high-flying New York fashion friend arrived in Seoul full of confidence a few years ago. She still asks me how she can break into the mainstream fashion circle. People with power constantly judge you and are wary of newcomers. While subculture crowds are very tightly bonded, they are still more open. They pay attention when someone new shows a distinctive sensibility or character.

When I met hip people in subculture while working at *Vogue*, I felt embarrassed and small to reveal my job, so I just said I worked in publishing. I don't really belong to high fashion. I enjoy subculture more.

## On the support system for K-fashion

We have so many designers ready for the 'Big Four' Fashion Weeks, with a clear identity. Seoul is getting much of the spotlight. However, managed by the government, which doesn't have a clue, Seoul Fashion Week continues to enforce absurd old rules. Leading designers even feel embarrassed to take part, so they put on their own shows instead. But only a few can afford it. Talented young

designers need a platform from which to showcase their work. From inexpensive raw material and accessories to great artisans making samples for you, Seoul offers a superior environment for manufacturing, producing clothes of great quality at reasonable costs. There are excellent photographers and videographers using the newest technology. How instantly brands use them up is so tragic. If they spot something new and cool, they ask creators to repeat it, making them quickly lose originality and competitiveness. Creators cannot say no, because they have to grab their chance before their work loses novelty.

## On copying in fashion

The new generation still copies a lot. Exposed to great things digitally, they've seen a lot and think they've got great style. But they lack the depth. It's superficial cool. Unlike us, having to prove ourselves through years of work to get to certain positions, people now decide their own title. To figure out whether they actually know something is quite time-consuming.

At the other end of the spectrum, there are increasingly outstanding talents, like home-grown brand PAF (Post Archive Faction). From clothes to visuals and editing, they exude global appeal with a distinctive language. Without leaving Korea, they were able to absorb what's cool and make it their own.

## On fashion magazines and K-style

Magazine covers create a buzz for rookie K-pop stars. Noticing the power of subculture and K-pop, *Vogue* has put down its untouchable pride to mingle in the real world. I helped *Vogue*'s persona to change from an impeccably dressed rich snob to a cool sassy woman happy to hang out with hip kids. Such a shift took place in *Vogue* Korea faster than in American *Vogue*.

instagram @xerianheu

# BAGO WOO

Founder of streetwear brand 99%IS-

## On his style and influences

Growing up with punk musicians, I have enjoyed creating concepts since I was a kid. Before my 'Yortsed' collection ('destroy' written backwards), I used to make clothes that looked cool in clubs, in the streets at night, in restrooms, when smoking. With 'Yortsed', I questioned why I needed to look for outside inspiration. I blew up clothes for the show (this left no clothes to show, which wasn't intentional). There have always been different movements reflecting an era, like Woodstock and hippy culture in the United States or reggae in Jamaica. I want to create my movement.

I have a punk mentality. People have said I am strange, crazy. What's important to me is what is different, special, us and now. Our slogan is 'I'm the 1% from the 99%'. 1% makes up for 99%.

I started to make clothes myself as a kid because I couldn't find what I liked to wear in Korea. It provided a base for me to start a brand. When I was thirteen, I wanted to wear common tartan-patterned trousers, so I drew the print onto white trousers with pen and crayon. When it rained, the colour bled, ruining my precious shoes.

## On his process and changing attitudes

I used to stitch or remake the clothes of musicians that I was following around. They urged me to go to a fashion school, saying that if I studied it properly at school, I could make them look cool. Afterwards, I didn't have friends studying fashion, I had no one to ask, so I had no other option but to try it out.

When I work, I cannot go out because there are so many things I need to create. I locked myself in a hotel room near my studio for seven months to finish my last collection. People complain that I don't do two collections a year, but I can't because it takes so long for me to create things by hand. In the past, I didn't want to be bothered by the world and tried to be a hermit away from people. But I realized I have a big responsibility to carry on my back. After people started to know me, I began to see that I was lucky to be able to influence others. Since 99%IS– started to have fans, we can now talk about 'our story'. My sixteenth collection is 'OUR STORY WiLL BE H1%STORY'.

## On trends

I read somewhere that Johnny Rotten from the Sex Pistols is known to have worn the first digital watch in the 1970s. Dr. Martens used the word 'air' before Nike and its tick. They were on time.

I'm not against trends or fashion. What I create is to become trends or fashion. Instead of trying to be stylish, style should naturally come out. And I want to express attitude. I show what we want and what's original to me. Instead of going to Hawaii to relax for a week to express the freedom of a summer night, or looking for inspiration somewhere outside, I seek inspiration from moments I create myself: I blew up clothes with a bomb, I let models walk the runway and put out a cigarette on a coat, I sat models on a car sliced down the middle to show a more sullen attitude on the runway. That's just my natural way of creation and expression.

## On living and working in Seoul

Growing up in Korea, I was so often told that I couldn't do something. It was very confusing. Why not? I have done it? I could do it?

I started making clothes in Japan. I only realized how much I was used to the Japanese way after moving back to Seoul. In Korea, they said that what I made was not clothes. They said I couldn't make clothes that looked like hospital clothing. I was just a strange kid with thick paint around my eyes. Korea was so full of things I should not do even before I tried. But I just did them without complaint, because I realized that there is a difference between things you must not do, and things no one has tried.

## On the rise of K-style

Like Japan and Tokyo style, the word naturally came out because there is already lots of interest in it, and in turn it attracts further interest. I'm curious how my brand and I can evolve K-style.

## On his next steps

I have a dream. I want to create a new word during my life. Based on our 'now', it will come out of music, food and play as well as fashion. With friends I've spent time with and new people I will meet, I will carry this out with more structure.

Regardless of what we are told not to do, we are going to take on challenges. The world I create can be a fun film, a tragic novel or a happy children's story. I simply live today for the day my dream will come true.

99percentis.com
instagram @99percentis

바조우

Kevin and Terrence Kim, founders of streetwear brand IISE

## On their style and influences

Terrence(T) and Kevin(K): Our mother is definitely one of our biggest influences. When we were young, she would always take us around New York to different museums, galleries and performances. She was also very interested in interior design, furniture and ceramic-making. She used to work at an agency in New York that imported some big European brands and I remember visiting her workplace several times and going through the racks of samples.

T: Personally, I really like classic wardrobe staples with modern detailing, and choose comfort and function as the most important elements. Brands like Jil Sander and Issey Miyake that our mother loved as well.

K: I just wear what's comfortable. I probably focus less on personal fashion and shopping because the majority of my time is thinking about fashion and designing for the brand. But I just end up wearing IISE anyway, so the brand and my own personal style are easily intertwined.

T: For IISE, what differentiated our approach compared to the previous generation of designers who attempted to interpret Korean traditions and aesthetics is our infusion of street culture. Not only the design was modernized, but the entire package of presenting it with hip-hop music, street styles and silhouettes, and even the visuals we created. Our very first video to showcase natural dyes had music that Kevin created by sampling traditional Korean instruments onto a hip-hop beat.

## On living and working in Seoul

T: Living in Seoul as Korean Americans has added to our strong sense of identity. We are always reminded that at the end of the day we are foreigners living in Korea, but how we approach and think about these experiences and translate them into our work is what makes IISE. There are real advantages to making clothes in Seoul. The infrastructure and proximity to all the fabric and hardware markets, manufacturers, samplers and designers make the entire process from design to final production extremely fast and relatively affordable compared to other major cities.

## On their brand and identity

K: Our brand's concept is Korean-inspired contemporary fashion. Most brands trying to do something Korean-inspired just reinvent

the hanbok or incorporate traditional art into a modern context. We have made a point that every collection and everything we do is inspired by Korea, and that forces us to always dig a level deeper by researching history and culture, much of which is relatively new to us.

T: When we first arrived in Korea in 2012, all of our visual inspiration came from our travels around the country. The bag collections we debuted with were made with traditional Korean fabrics that were naturally dyed and had some design details inspired by the strapless bags that Buddhist monks carry. The hardware we decided to use on our bags were drawer handles for traditional Korean furniture. It was a very copy-and-paste method, but executed in a new way.

After living in Korea for longer, we drew our inspirations from daily Seoul life. Our daily commute to work passed through the Gyeongbokgung Palace area, where we witnessed protests happening every day for years. We observed both what the protestors and the police were wearing and designed pieces inspired by both parties.

K: Our Fall/Winter 2021 collection was based on our take on Korean workwear, which is quite different from in the US It all has to do with what's available in Korea at a cheaper price. For instance, carrier service guys wear a combination of hiking gear and polo shirts. They amend their gear themselves by patching motorcycle tags to their pants and jackets. We think they are the most stylish people in Seoul. Korea wants to present a cleaner and more modern version of itself internationally. The service guys are tucked under the carpet, but we feel they are more interesting. They are the backbone of the blue-collar labour force, and the city cannot run without these people.

T:     Being born and raised in America and becoming adults living in Korea for the past eight years has shaped us and the brand. If we create something 'too Korean', then it's perceived as very old school and boring. On the flip side, if it does not contain some Korean element, it may look too westernized and nothing special.

When we first started visiting older markets around Seoul, we were surprised to see some stalls selling naturally dyed fabrics. The colour, texture and processes were so interesting and we wanted to start using them. This led us to the vendors, who would then connect us to the fabric suppliers and the natural dyers. We would visit these artisans in the countryside and they would always be surprised that two American brothers were interested in learning more about their craft. They would not only help us in every way, but also feed us and tell us stories about their past and how they came to practise natural dyeing.

## On the rise of K-style

T:     Seoul is a city that is evolving every year. When we first started here, we weren't really fans of existing brands here, but there are so many great brands that have sprung up over the past couple of years. The city has so much energy and is so technologically advanced that anything spreads quickly through the youth.

K:     The emergence of K-fashion is also the direct product of people of my generation and younger having the luxury of being able to pursue art, fashion and culture. Korea is a relatively newly rich country, so we're later to the fashion game in a global context, and so it makes sense that K-style is something that we see emerging now.

T:     K-style is a reflection of Seoul, always changing, adopting, improving, so it is hard to pinpoint exactly, but that is also what makes it so exciting.

K:     Korean fashion is in the best place it has ever been. To be honest, there are not many reference points for people to refer to Korean fashion or Korean inspiration in the modern context. I really feel like we're at the beginning of shaping what that is in a modern and global context. All of the designers here are shaping that narrative.

iise.co
instagram @terrencetk @kevnkim @iiseseoul

KOREAN COOL

KOREAN COOL

KOREAN COOL

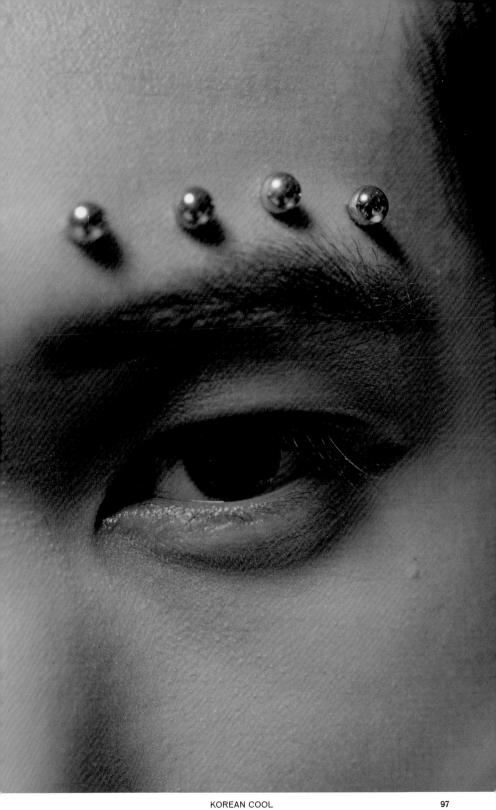

KOREAN COOL

KOREAN COOL

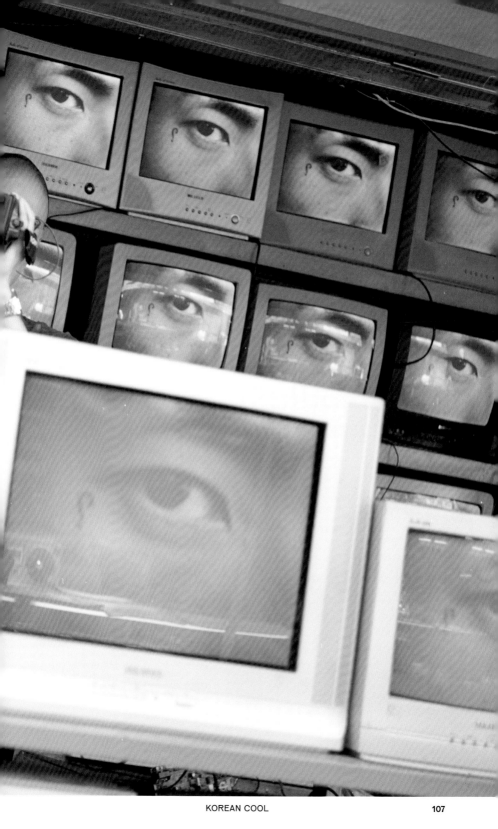

KOREAN COOL

KOREAN COOL

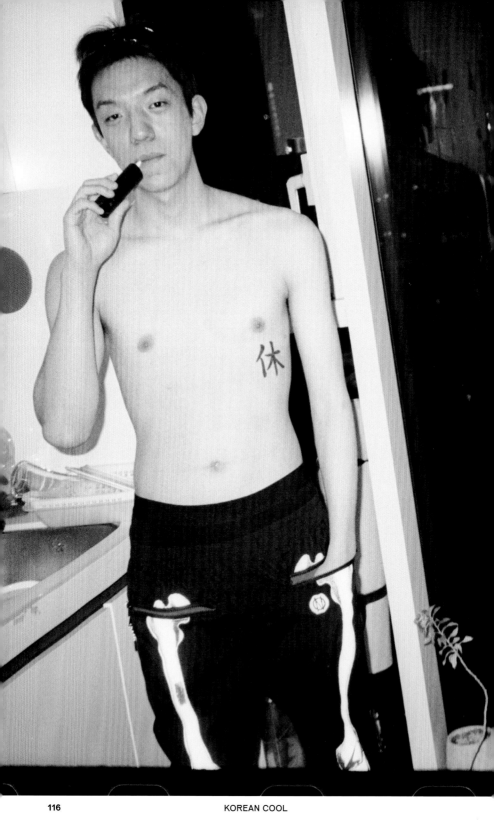

# Nana Youngnam
# 영롱킴 Long Kim

Drag performer and YouTuber changing attitudes
to the LGBTQ+ community

## On his style and influences

The older generation of drag performers inspires me. They have long-lasting fans who are getting old with them, sharing memories and stories. It gives me butterflies imagining growing old with my fans.

I have thousands of different looks. For a photoshoot in *The Musical* magazine, I turned myself into Simba (Lion King's girlfriend). My signature style involves wearing custom clothes that accentuate my tattoos and short hair, which is unusual for drag artists in Korea. On stage, I take motifs from pop divas of the eighties and nineties, adding something unique to Nana.

Most Korean drag performers care about being feminine and only post images with full make-up. I'm not afraid of appearing with no make-up. I like building a masculine body, so I post pictures of myself sweating in the gym. My peers complain about it just because they can't do it and are jealous. Pfft!

## On developing a strong sense of identity

Instead of sticking to typical drag make-up, I like exploring more multidimensional, painting-like or grotesque looks. Amidst beautiful and popular looks, I suddenly appear as totally weird, evil, an animalistic or non-human object, which amuses people. When Byredo recruited me as a model, I noticed the make-up package had a cheeky and distinctive look, so I made myself up to look like a package.

Drag itself comes as a shock, so why would I hesitate to try something new? Of course, people's reactions matter. I like being famous because people are more accepting, but it won't cease to be challenging.

나나영롱킴

## On living and working in Seoul

I moved to Seoul from Busan at twenty, seeking a proper queer life that is only possible here. Seoul is fascinating. Amazing art appears on the walls. Many talented musicians busk on the street. Drag artists like me are passionately entertaining from the underground.

## On drag and changing attitudes to the LGBTQ+ community in Korea

When I was setting myself up as a drag artist, I had no means to promote myself. I visited clubs disguised as a customer to seek work. 'I could pick up the mood by making a dramatic entrance,' I claimed to managers. Now, with YouTube and Instagram, I can take ownership, fully express myself and expand boundaries. Launching Nana TV on YouTube, I rapidly built an overseas fanbase by offering subtitles in English, Japanese and Portuguese (for Brazilian fans).

I got dumped by my boyfriend when he found out I had started drag. Other gays poured curses on me when I kept my drag outfit on when going to a club. They ranted that because of gay people like me, they got negative attention while they desperately tried to be under the radar. They were afraid that a loud gay like me might cause them harm. Most gay people are still not out in Korea, so you need to be careful not to disclose their secrets. But these days, guys ask me out because I do drag. They love to take pictures with me in clubs.

A leading Korean beauty brand, Hera, asked me to co-develop a limited-edition make-up line in 2020. The company used to be conservative; I am the first LGBTQ+ person to collaborate with them. Friends who are not out have told me that their female colleagues watch Nana TV all the time and can't stop talking about how much they adore me. They've thanked me for making being gay look cool. I am proud to help them feel less ashamed and open up with pride. Straight people are starting to accept different expressions of sexuality and gender.

In Korea, many people in their twenties still follow a typical route of going to university, relying on their parents, getting a job and marrying at a certain age. They are not bold enough to take risks. They treasure me because they live vicariously through me.

## On the rise of K-style

In the early 2000s, foreigners only knew Korea as a country near Japan and China. Now, thanks to K-style, they want to visit Korea. With K-pop's popularity, its queer fans naturally got curious about queer life in Korea and discovered me through K-pop music videos. Because of K-beauty's fame, overseas fans want to know the secret of how my smooth and trouble-free skin wins over thick drag makeup.

I mix lots of Korean songs into my repertoire, because I feel that's a good way to add K-style to my shows.

## On hopes for the future

I refuse to set goals for the future. If you set a finishing line and only focus on reaching it, you miss out on precious things, including

나나영롱킴

the people around you. I got here because I didn't care about being successful and famous. I just tried new things that I felt I could have fun with.

In Korea, people care about being at the top too much. I often receive messages from young boys who are struggling at school. I tell them, 'Don't despair! You can be successful in your own way!'

instagram @nana_youngrongkim

# Mischief퍼스치프

Jieun Seo and Jiyoon Jung, founders of streetwear brand Mischief

## On their style and influences

When we started, we were inspired by nineties hip-hop musicians with a big influence in subculture, such as Mos Def, Souls of Mischief and The Pharcyde. We thought it would be more interesting for Korean women to reinterpret these looks, but we felt inadequate.

We wanted to express Korea and Asia through our own perspectives. As we grew more confident, we drew inspiration from our surroundings and Korean flavour. We even find Admiral Yi Sun-sin's statue in Gwanghwamun Plaza chic. We are using traditional materials typically used for *hanbok*, and have reinterpreted *norigae*, the typical traditional accessory for *hanbok*.

We went to lots of parties by DJ group 360 Sounds and met so many great artists with similar tastes who have been instrumental for Mischief. We always like to explore something fun. We get inspired by close friends' new work, and often come up with witty projects through casual chats with friends working in different sectors. Recently, we approached Lim Kim because we liked her path and identity. For Women's Day, she wrote a song for us, and we designed clothes and produced visuals and a music video.

We both like just doing things without formal structures. We are self-assured. No fear stopped us from launching Mischief without any experience or overseas studying. Like our brand name, being too serious or seeking meaning for everything doesn't suit us. We like positivity, fun and expressing ourselves directly without metaphor. Whatever we do should feel natural.

Because of the tough and raw images in our design, visuals and music, we have always been known as gritty. But underneath lies something elegant. We started casual clothing with a hint of classic, and have tried to infuse sophistication throughout.

## On Mischief's values

We only make clothes we want to wear. We want cool, confident, proud people to wear our brand. Many women tell us they wear our brand because they aspire to be that person. We put significant effort into spreading our culture. We want customers to understand what we like, what we want to talk about and why we make what we do.

We started out wanting to share the music and clothes we enjoyed, and put lyrics from our favourite songs on our clothes. Gradually we started to include strong messages of our own. For sustainability, we try to avoid launching new collections or products without a purpose. Our first products were bags made by upcycling clothes. We collaborate with young artists to rework our existing lines. We don't necessarily look socially conscious, so if we show that a brand like us cares, it might have a positive impact.

We also want to correct a misinterpretation of feminism in Korea. In male-dominated street culture, we benefitted because we stood out as women. Instead of shouting that we were weak, we wanted to convey female strength and coolness. However, we realized we need to talk about prevailing gender inequality. We learned that people often commit wrongs because they don't know better, so we want to share what we know to make a change.

## On living and working in Seoul

Seoul is a small city where it takes one degree of separation to reach anybody you want to meet. You can easily become friends with people in diverse fields. It offers a fun environment in which to work. People visiting Seoul are amused that everyone is friends.

Korea is claiming international recognition. People on the inside feel it arrived rather late, so everyone is charged and sprinting together to the peak.

## On female subculture scenes

Over the last few years we have put lots of effort into gathering a female crew, to show that there are many dashing women making marks in diverse sectors, from music to dancing to design. Lim Kim, Kyuhee Baik and the Dadaism girls all continue to present fascinating work. Now there are more young women than men in subculture. A distinct solidarity exists. They want to express a clear identity and pride as women. Young women who were not interested in subculture might now be attracted to it because women are doing it.

## On music

Music completes our work by delivering the mood. If you match a very feminine dress with hardcore hip-hop music, it adds a different vibe. Mischief represents hip-hop culture. We like the confident and unflinching attitude of people who do or like hip-hop. We don't hire professional models, and work with our friends instead. At photoshoots, we tell them, 'Bring out your hip-hop attitude.' We want them to show themselves instead of trying to make our clothes pretty.

## On the rise of K-style

Pioneers like 360 Sounds built cool communities in subculture through music. A collective of DJs, they had diverse members, including photographers, a skateboarder, rappers. They threw the coolest parties in town. People from New York or London were impressed to find such parties in Seoul.

Young people are much more diverse and carry out ideas more easily. We used to think we had to prepare everything properly before showing it at once. These days, social media makes it so easy to present even simple and small things you have made.

A strong subculture helps drive the mainstream of K-style. Young producers around us have started to work on K-pop, making it astounding. In the past, K-pop idols only wore Mischief if a stylist who was interested in subculture chose it. Increasingly, idols pick it themselves, as they develop their own interest in subculture. It has brought more collaboration with them. It's natural for mainstream K-pop to look for something new and cool, and the boundary between subculture and mainstream culture gets blurry.

K-pop made Korean style internationally known. Lots of our international fans are interested in K-culture. It feels rather silly to apply 'K' so randomly, but it's a way of branding. If we are seen as illustrating Korean flavour, that's cool. Our biggest overseas fans are Japanese. They used to look down on Korean fashion because Tokyo was considered far ahead of Seoul. Now, it helps that we are from Korea.

mischief.co.kr
instagram @mischiefmakers

# Kyuhee 백규희 Baik

**Head of Stüssy Korea and Director of Strategy at Hyein Seo**

## On her style and influences

Over the past ten years, I've participated in and watched various circles of subcultures, which have influenced my sense of style. The cultural environment surrounding me is a reflection of my style. This was heavily triggered through music, specifically in clubs and nightlife when I was younger. I met a lot of my friends at clubs when I first moved to Seoul.

My style is about comfort above anything else. If I don't feel comfortable, I don't feel like myself. As for my work, I don't work with brands that I personally cannot relate to. I have been fortunate enough to work with brands that are stylistically and culturally related to my personal interests.

My work is an extension of my background in anthropology and the ability to observe and understand behaviour. When I first arrived in Seoul, I was examining creative behaviour in hip-hop clubs. I would watch people change or break social conventions to express themselves and later make relationships and connections through that. A lot of my work opportunities come from relationships that started in underground clubs. Having met in a context of shared interest, I think there is an authentic sense of trust that is crucial to growing a brand and understanding a culture.

## On living and working in Seoul

Seoul is extremely fast-paced and requires you to be constantly informed. Media is a huge proponent of accelerated cultural consumption, whether it be television, social media, texting, mobile

백규희

applications. It's actually quite a lot of pressure. It's easy to fall behind if you don't know what's going on all the time here, which is why you're kind of required to be so connected.

## On the rise of K-style

Being so digitally connected, Seoul has become an ever more relevant, global player across various industries, from film and beauty to music, fashion and food. A larger, more general interest in Asia is inevitable due to the importance of modern markets and economies (and therefore cultural influence) shifting from West to East.

K-style follows an institution of commercializing Korean culture. It is a recent trend to add a 'K' in front of various industries to define contemporary Korean culture for the wider audience. I don't think there are specific parameters to define K-style, besides a trend or look coming from Korea that attracts global interest in it. Take, for instance, K-beauty and the 'Korean 10-step beauty manual': the ritual of perfect skin and prioritizing skincare is a long-standing practice that has garnered global attention over the past several years. Who hasn't tried a sheet mask these days?

As with any mass culture, you can find K-style's roots in subculture. When you consider K-pop, you could say it was born from underground club culture in the late 1980s. Back then, there was a small niche of breakdancing at clubs in Itaewon that were intended for the US military. This was the transmission of hip-hop subculture to Korean mass culture, as a few of those dancers became members of Seo Taiji and Boys, a group considered to be foundational to modern K-pop. Members of the group would go on to become K-pop moguls, one of them the founder of YG Entertainment.

## On club culture

The sociologist Dick Hebdige neatly defines a subculture as 'a subversion to normalcy' that '[brings] together like-minded individuals...to develop a sense of identity'. When I think of nightlife and clubbing, style and behaviour are strongly intertwined outlets of self-expression.

Foremost, the setting of a club is quite different from my day-to-day. It is the individuals that participate that make the charm and spontaneity inherent in a club. My style of dress could change if I wanted, the dimly lit setting allowed me to feel more comfortable in showing more skin or wearing darker make-up. Some may dress more eccentrically or provocatively. People going to a club will share their interest in music and also a sort of similarity in how they dress. I think a lot of people who club have an unconventional style. There is a level of comfort in being among those who stray from convention.

The club scene is very energetic and expressive. The club is a context where people can release themselves from societal norms and pressure.

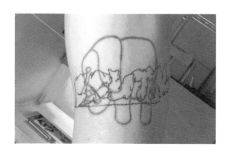

백규희

## On the consumption of subculture

Displays of distinction over conformity are a recent phenomenon among Korean youth. Whereas before, mass communications channels like television defined taste and style for a general audience, the advent of social media, especially Instagram, has allowed a more democratic stage for self-expression and networking. Basically, social media granted the gathering and sharing of any and every little subversion of or diversion from mass culture. Korean youth are extremely internet-savvy and constantly connected, which results in instantaneous consumption and production of culture.

The biggest change in subculture is being able to see it on social media at any time and in any place. While social media can be a platform to bring like-minded individuals together, it can also dilute and over-expose their unique connection. I think the increasingly rapid rate at which subcultures become commercialized through such uncontrollable exposure can be detrimental. It essentially kills it that much more quickly. But the process is cyclical — it can also incubate more and more facets of subculture.

instagram @floss_everyday

'*Monocle* has long been fascinated with Korean style, and the power and influence of Korean music and technology in the hands of the nation's experimental youth. But K-style doesn't stop there -- from seniors on the golf course to young actors going global, there's a commitment and inventiveness that endlessly intrigues. We recognize all the elements, but in their assembly something special happens.'

— Andrew Tuck, Editor-in-Chief, *Monocle*

LANDSCAPE, CITYSCAPE

LANDSCAPE, CITYSCAPE

LANDSCAPE, CITYSCAPE

LANDSCAPE, CITYSCAPE

LANDSCAPE, CITYSCAPE

LANDSCAPE, CITYSCAPE

LANDSCAPE, CITYSCAPE

LANDSCAPE, CITYSCAPE

LANDSCAPE, CITYSCAPE

LANDSCAPE, CITYSCAPE

# Te 양태오 Yang

## Asia's leading interior designer

## On his style and influences

I am inspired by artist Lee Ufan and architects Choi Wook and Seung H. Sang. The critic Choi Bum strongly influenced my design philosophy. He taught me that designers are shaping the future and should be conscious, responsible and autonomous. He showed me where I am and where Korean design stands.

I believe my personal style has a big impact on my work. I push myself to read widely in order to stay up to date with what's contemporary, but I avoid wearing trendy things because I worry it will make my work feel that way. I wear clothes in black and grey and mix them with the latest sneakers by Virgil Abloh.

Being original in my work is based on deep understanding. People keep copying and move further and further from originality and a distinctive identity. I develop my own voice through intensive studying and internalizing what I have learned. It is painstaking work to finely chop what I learn, conceptualize it, turn it into a project goal and choose keywords to communicate it to my staff and clients.

## On living and working in Seoul

With its huge population, Seoul becomes a situational play that forces development and innovation based on thoughts and visual elements derived from so many people. Designers cannot be idle. You are bound to fall behind and disappear if you merely produce something pretty. You might end up churning out commercial work that becomes waste.

양태오

Seoul trained me to stand steady and strive to discover something original while fighting the big tides driven by trends and commercial success. I constantly try to find a balance between local heritage and what's contemporary. Seoul went through modernization driven by external forces, which resulted in big gaps and voids. It's a privilege for designers to fill that void.

## On infusing Korean traditions and aesthetics with contemporary design

On returning to Korea to set up a studio after studying abroad, I started out designing pretty spaces that pleased clients. That changed when I moved to a traditional house, a *hanok*, in Bukchon, the oldest neighbourhood in Seoul. I was impressed by the wisdom and beauty of Korean tradition, and it ignited a deep curiosity about traditional aesthetics. I saw how *hanok* were becoming trendy even as they were being demolished to make room for more commercial makeovers.

It pushed me to steep local value and heritage in modernity through new interpretations. Armed with new convictions, I let go of projects looking for pretty features and built up a portfolio supporting my beliefs. In my practice, I want to reinterpret the Joseon Dynasty's aesthetics with a contemporary take, to introduce a new K-style focusing on substance and a spiritual side.

'Mu-mee' can be described as beyond taste. It goes beyond all tastes and looks at the essence. It was manifested in white porcelain moon jars, and in the spaces in Dosan Seowon, the Confucian academy, where nothing was placed or added. Through our Mu-mee-based furniture line, we bring high-brow craft down to simple design.

We use *nubim*, a traditional cotton used for blankets, as a fabric for a chair covering. Instead of imposing tradition, we adapt it to create a new luxury and lifestyle.

## On the rise of K-style

With such a concentration of people, fierce competition has been inherent to Seoul. Following rapid economic development, the focus of that competition has shifted to culture. I feel it's both a blessing and a curse that people can check out designers' work so easily through social media. Designers need to stop competing to make pretty things. Designers should make a statement, advocate it, and solve problems.

The growth of K-style has been a gradual process, like Dansaekhwa in the 1970s and 1980s, which has been popular on the international art scene for a long time.

K-style has only just begun. It is in search of its identity. We have seen a lot of evidence that something genuinely Korean and specific to us can garner international interest. Finding a balance within imbalance, between tradition and the contemporary, passive and active, will further establish K-style. Now that we have more designers focusing on their core values and delving into the social dimensions of design, I expect K-style to become deeper and stronger.

## On his **EATH LIBRARY** skincare brand

I wanted to focus on what's missing from K-style. While K-beauty entails some mystique, it is mainly associated with immediate results and cheap prices. Instead, we are about the essence of Korean medicine and its serene lifestyle.

Traditional Korean medicine cures people through mind, essence and a nature-friendly lifestyle. I recalled childhood memories of a traditional Korean medicine clinic, which felt like a small, warm library with old books and a subtle scent of herbal tea. So I created a showroom where people can come to relax in the middle of the bustling city with a warm tea and music.

We don't produce the disposable face-mask packs that made K-beauty popular globally, because of their negative impact on the environment. Many customers say they chose our overnight mask because it doesn't produce any waste. We are participating in changing consumers' behaviour in a positive way, which is rewarding.

## On next steps

While reinterpreting Korean aesthetics was a starting point for me, I have moved to create an international language. I'm studying time travel to come up with a new fragrance line. The concept is to record moments and time through scents.

teoyangstudio.com
instagram @teoyang

# Kwangho이광호ee

**Artist and designer who paved the way for collectible Korean design**

## On his style and influences

I used to be influenced by my favourite artists. Now I'm more inspired by my surroundings, family and friends. I began to value people who persevere through their work. When I became a father, my focus shifted, and I became interested in an honest, authentic life that suits my work.

In my personal style, I expressed myself by adding accessories such as jewelry and thick-framed glasses. I have fewer decorative things now that my attitude has moved towards clearing out material things. I enjoy comfortable outfits in distinctive colours and characterful materials, or old clothes, to feel the passage of time. I'll wear workwear for installation days, but whether I'm working or playing with my kids, my style doesn't really change.

I like 'simplicity within complexity'. While it doesn't stand out from far away, the authenticity and the power of the material are felt when you come close.

In my work, style begins with curiosity. The process of finding my favourite shape, proportion and use of the material through numerous iterations constitutes the basic framework. Inevitably, all the works in my exhibitions are part of a series. My weaving works result from fifteen years of iteration.

## On living in Seoul and moving to Jeju Island

I am Korean to my bones. I grew up in the countryside, which went through typical urbanization near Seoul. Friends I associate with can be very Korean, and these relationships form the core of my being. Now that I've moved to Jeju Island, which is closer to nature,

I expect to encounter the true Korea even more intensely. Short overseas trips awaken my senses to my home country. Looking out from the plane approaching Seoul, walking out of the airport to the different smells, I always feel at home. I discover wonderful things that were too familiar to me to notice before.

## On the rise of K-style

A new confidence combined with Koreans' strong desire to out-perform has had a big impact. When I started my studio, everyone thought you had to go to art college and go abroad to study and work. Now young people just get it done.

You can also show your work immediately. We call it the 'Korean explosion' among designer friends. If we make something, we tend to get an instant call from overseas. Young people form groups and bring in friends from the music and fashion scenes. I could complete a project for a large space by gathering architects and interior designer friends.

It feels a bit forced to pinpoint exactly what K-style is. I think the timing was just right in many sectors, but it's impossible to break it down and explain each part.

Looking at my field, I feel Koreans excel in craftsmanship and sensitivity. Combined with the right timing and technology, we have been able to present our work more actively. Koreans love to beat others and boast about it. We put bigger signage on our shops, quickly expand our businesses through franchising and yearn for recognition. I think it has all led to an explosive change.

## On Korean aesthetics in his work

If I felt foreign standards mattered, I might have tried to express 'Korean-ness' more dramatically, but I never intended to. I don't represent Korea, and I don't intentionally melt something Korean into my work. Claiming that I do would make me feel dishonest and inauthentic. Instead, I just feel that Korea is already deep inside me.

## On young Koreans' newfound cultural confidence

Before social media, we couldn't see how our peers were growing. Going to the marvellous exhibition of a famous foreign designer in his forties, I couldn't glimpse the mistakes or regrettable decisions he made in his twenties and see how he overcame adversity. Looking at impressive final results without understanding the process, we were left with nothing but compulsion and impatience. But now people can see what their peers in far-away countries are working on and realize that what we are grappling with isn't that different from them. It leads us to feel that our work isn't too bad to show. It encourages young people to become more active in trying something.

## On working in Seongsu-dong, and the changes happening there

I witnessed how my neighbourhood in Seoul, Seongsu-dong, became cool and sophisticated by rapidly absorbing foreign styles, including those from Japan. I feel the emergence of K-style is similar to Seongsu's transformation.

The regeneration of factories, the foundation of Korea's modernization, into surprisingly hip places to host sophisticated programmes has created a great buzz. Seongsu's unique sense of the present intertwined with the past shows us the potential for the future. The headquarters of large entertainment labels have moved there from Gangnam, and Seongsu keeps going through changes, encompassing the commercial, art and design worlds. That's also happening with K-style. In Korea, when a certain neighbourhood becomes hip, other districts and even other cities tend to shamelessly copy the name and the mood of the street, and pretend to be something else instead of their own locality. Like the pursuit of locality in Seongsu, I believe K-style needs to bring something of its own to be able to grow.

'Upward levelling' worries me. Most people strive towards better design because they have seen enough and are determined to beat the competition. But they don't go further. In 2021, Bauhaus and Wassily chairs were so popular that every cool café and shop in Seongsu looked identical. In order for a space to be exceptional, regardless of attracting a crowd, it should care about something beyond what people can see.

Synergy only happens when there are enough places with a distinctive concept and interesting story. We will see more themes coming out of K-style only if more people push its boundaries.

Something feels truly remarkable when it goes beyond the public's expectations and gives those who notice a truly thrilling experience. When you travel to Japan, you stumble across special spaces of all different sizes, often in totally unexpected alleys. Like Kyoto and Tokyo style, I look forward to Seoul and Seongsu style emerging.

kwangholee.com
instagram @_kwangho_lee

# Mingoo 강민구 Kang

Chef who pioneered New Korean Dining
at his flagship restaurant Mingles

## On his style and influences

It hasn't been that long since I realized I needed to learn Korean cuisine. Because Korean food was so familiar to me living in Korea, I thought I could make Korean food in my own way, but I was wrong. Working abroad made me aware that I needed fundamental teaching in Korean food.

I learned from Buddhist nun Jeong Kwan and chef Cho Hee-sook (the recipient of Asia's Best Female Chef 2020); I learned the attitude of a Korean chef from Chef Cho, and the essence of the boundless world of fermented vegetables from Nun Jeong. I learned that Korean food on its own can be diverse and creative, without adding any foreign ingredients.

In my restaurant, we respect the origins of Korean food but present it with today's technology and sensibility. I think our identity has become more distinct as the team members and the chef keep developing, exploring and working hard, in line with the social atmosphere and what interests us.

I don't try to create something particularly new, something out of this world or exceptionally creative. Instead, I cook what I am interested in and what I find delicious. I try to keep the characteristics of Korean cuisine as a base, while expressing something that hasn't been commonly tried. I think that may be why Mingles's food gets recognized for being at once new and familiar.

## On living and working in Seoul

At first, I had a desire to open a restaurant in a big city abroad. However, as the world became smaller and Seoul became internationally attractive, I no longer thought that I had to go overseas to introduce Korean food. Seoul presents you with abundant support from Korean staff and local customers. In fact, being in Korea allows us to use Korean ingredients and work with staff with a deep understanding of our culture, which makes us distinct. Starting in Seoul meant I had a good foundation when it came to opening a restaurant in Hong Kong, called Hansik Goo.

## On the rise of K-style

K-style can be summed up as forward-looking, entrepreneurial, trendy and expanding. A past of many conflicts and rapid growth gave birth to Korean's future-orientated thinking.

I think it is the style that best reflects the changing world in the current generation. Although Korea is a small country, it has become a test bed for what's cool worldwide; perhaps a testimony to its global sensibility.

## On the attraction of Korean food

If you have very good ingredients, the answer to cooking is already there. With good ingredients, a simple recipe that preserves their taste can be closest to the answer — for example, in Japanese food, the ingredients are the destination of the dish. There is a limit to what can be added. On the other hand, there are many things that can be added to Korean food. You can create countless combinations by mixing various kinds of sauces and spices, such as red chilli pepper paste, soybean paste, soy sauce and garlic. Korean food lets you express your own colours with good ingredients.

## On changes on the Korean dining scene and New Korean Dining

When I first started cooking, I was often told I should cook what the market and customers wanted, not what I wanted. However, since 2013, when I began running Mingles, the space I have carved out has slowly come to be supported, respected and loved. I think Seoul customers' food tastes and acceptance of new cultures have strengthened. Korea's food culture has developed fast, in particular in the casual dining scene.

What turned out to be very challenging was that none other than Koreans were the most conservative and most critical of this new type of Korean food. But expanding the possibilities and boundaries of Korean food has been most fulfilling and fun. Presenting something new can be important, but introducing what we already had felt even more innovative. I try to bring out what can be fresh and enchanting from food in our daily life.

## On his fried chicken brand Hyodo Chicken

I created it with my dear friend Shin Chang-ho of the restaurant Joo Ok. As fine dining chefs dealing only with very few guests, we wanted to connect more widely through a dish the public adores, and which I often enjoy. I think Korea is good at mixing cultures from outside and making it our own. While maintaining the Korean sensibility and taste, we wanted to make our recipe similar to the original fried chicken, since there is a difference between fried chicken and KFC (Korean Fried Chicken).

Since most fried chicken in Korea is made from commercially available factory-produced bases, there is inevitably a limit to the taste. From making the sauce to marinating the chickens, our chicken is finished off by the delicate hands of chefs and cooks. We also use ingredients that are not typical of fried chicken, such as local green pepper, anchovies and lotus root. Presenting a familiar yet refreshing food culture directly from our hands is our brand identity.

강민구

## On Korean comfort food

Korean food as a comfort food enables it to attract attention in fine dining. New Korean Dining is based on traditional and everyday Korean food taken up a notch, so getting used to the idea of Korean food as a comfort food is necessary to understand it more deeply.

I believe the world of food can become deeper and more vivid when we understand food as a stem of culture.

restaurant-mingles.com
hansikgoo.hk
instagram @mingleseoul @hyodochicken

'The validity of the term "K-style" has yet to be discovered. This process of finding an identity between globalization and localization can support other cultures' stories.'

— DJ Soulscape (Min Jun Park), creative director, composer, producer and founder of 360 Sounds

FROM THE STUDIO TO THE STREET

FROM THE STUDIO TO THE STREET

FROM THE STUDIO TO THE STREET

FROM THE STUDIO TO THE STREET

FROM THE STUDIO TO THE STREET

FROM THE STUDIO TO THE STREET

FROM THE STUDIO TO THE STREET

FROM THE STUDIO TO THE STREET

2. 8.18

FROM THE STUDIO TO THE STREET

FROM THE STUDIO TO THE STREET

FROM THE STUDIO TO THE STREET

FROM THE STUDIO TO THE STREET

FROM THE STUDIO TO THE STREET

# 황Hwang
# Soyoon소윤

Solo musician and leader of rock band Se So Neon

## On her style and influences

I like people whose work matches how they express themselves. I question why people wear the same clothes everyone else wears. You can express your personality, energy and preferences through fashion. But people choose fashion to show off or to be recognized by others, which is no fun.

I feel a strange attraction towards elderly people. They don't wear clothes dictated by the mainstream culture. They put on whatever they feel like; tuck an entire jacket inside your trousers, wear a vest over it, select an odd colour combination. Their fashion looks most chic.

My everyday fashion tends to be neat and clean-cut with matching clothes, jeans and comfortable sneakers.

I change my look as a musician according to the song, situation and the image I project. I keep my style void and absorb whatever colour I put on with ease. My work extends to fashion, so I keep it fresh and changing, melting my vision into it. I can be really low-key or stunning. Fans seem to associate me with wearing glasses and playing guitar. I do have bad eyesight, but I also like that glasses are not typically seen in Korean mass media.

As a creative director, I come up with all the visuals and atmosphere, from uploaded photos to a music video's texture, to my fashion style. Creating a song is like dandelion seeds flying off and falling to the ground. A song goes through many processes before finding roots and blooming. The actual writing comes easily. I visualize the atmosphere, senses and colours that occurred and share it with my band members and staff. As I follow my intuition and gather people together to create something, it crystallizes.

황소윤

## On living and working in Seoul

I grew up surrounded by nature and only started fully experiencing Seoul as an adult. I am one of those random people who didn't choose it. I don't feel I belong here. Seoul is so dense, overly stimulating and fast. I'm forced to see things that are violent, one-sided and unjust. I can't really ignore them because I am supposed to be fully awake as an artist. I feel a lot of coldness from Seoul, which is reflected in my music.

I always look at strangers, old people, hawkers and labourers who are cast to society's fringes. People who are on the brink of survival comfort and inspire me. I find it uncomfortable to sing in a mainstream style, but these people are probably the true mainstream.

## On the rise of K-style

Even though time has moved on and what was previously suppressed is accepted, people are less courageous because they are more conscious of others' perception. The way young people express themselves is not diverse or impressive. Narrow-minded education and surroundings inevitably limit us. But I see gradual progress. In 2020, a member of parliament showing up to an official session in a dress caused much criticism and debate. In the 2010s, queer culture was considered embarrassing; now, so many TV programmes show it (even though it's still not consumed very naturally).

People are still not used to expressing themselves through fashion. When they dress up for work, they still worry about sticking out. At the level of mass culture, I don't think K-style is distinct yet. It seems to be enjoyed by a small circle of K-pop idols and artists.

**On different identities as Se So Neon's leader and solo musician So! YoON!**

They have drastically different languages. Se So Neon keeps the record of my life. The band is much more difficult because of tensions among members, but I love it because of the energy, comradeship and fun I get from the other members. So!YoOn! is an exploration to let out a new me. It satisfies musical desires I cannot express in Se So Neon.

**On being a female band leader in Korea**

I resist being objectified. I just express what I like. I want to be understood as I am. I only recognized myself as a woman after starting my music career and being called a female rocker. Ever since I was very little, I have wanted to show what's beyond a category or a tag. My female fans tell me they get courage and comfort from me, and I have come to accept that if I can encourage others as a woman, it's cool.

**On Korean music scenes and being an indie musician**

In Korea, the boundary between 'indie' and 'major' has broken down. It is hard to survive as an indie musician in Korea, but you can quickly move 'overground' if you have commercial values. When we started, we played small basement stages in the Hongdae clubs. People stopped going to underground clubs, and now bands need to be much more commercial. We don't set boundaries because we don't want to limit ourselves. We performed a song called 'Jayu' (Freedom) that was considered unsuitable for mainstream tastes on a mainstream TV show made for K-pop idols. We found it exciting to break through that boundary.

I wish people were allowed to flow with their own tempo. The music industry moves too fast. There are so many things you cannot do. None of my favourite musicians make it to the mainstream. I am curious about how much I can persuade people without compromising. Instead of using additives to make everyone like my food, I want to present the most delicious food that I like.

## On future plans

I leave plenty of space for how I will express myself in the future, because I became a musician only by chance. I made a demo with the songs I wrote at high school and sent them around to see the reaction. Recently, I launched a limited edition of glassware. I'm interested in creating beauty products that are natural, healthy and environmentally friendly. I have always thought art is integrated, whether it's music or fashion. I want to continue expanding myself with an open mind.

instagram @sleeep_sheeep @se_so_neon

Pioneer of the K-style tattoo and the head of Korea's tattooists' union

## On his style and influences

I collect paintings, photographs, images from fashion and nature that
are relevant to my tattoos' direction and texture and refer to them
constantly. A tattoo isn't a picture you can take down to storage.
My inspiration stays with my client forever through my work, so
I choose light, life and love as themes.

I approach my work like fine art, so I position myself as an
artist rather than looking rough or hip. How I'm dressed, talk, walk
and perform constitute the whole experience of the tattoo. I believe
in presenting a memorable style, instead of looking like your uncle
or a guy next door.

I chose human skin for a canvas, needles for brushes and
ink for paints, and I have been pushing boundaries with these
materials. I started what's now called fine tattoo, a name I proposed
at international tattoo competitions in Asia when I was part of the
juries, and which is now widely used.

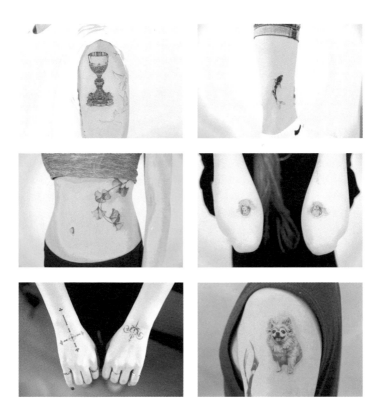

## On his working process

Figuring out what will look beautiful when illustrated on a moving body is important. Our bodies are made up of large and small shapes that change as we move. It's more complicated than working on a piece of paper.

I encourage interaction with the client by discussing the purpose and the tone of design, which clients like because it makes the tattoo feel more their own.

## On living and working in Seoul

The coolest aspect of Seoul is that its remarkable speed of change has transformed into its energy as a city, quickly addressing discrimination and prejudice and creating new rules.

Without a medical licence, working as a tattooist is illegal here. Because tattoos were perceived as part of a culture of organized crime, the government didn't want tattoo culture to spread. We had to create a totally new style and process in order to overcome the absurdity caused by the Korean law. Interestingly, such progress is now bringing dynamic changes into other sectors.

## On the emergence of K-style

Korea has a history common among East Asian countries, involving colonization, civil war and a series of military dictatorships. Through hardship and political turmoil, Koreans have accumulated memories of hard-earned victories. The dynamic speed of political and social change in Korea has developed its cultural influence.

Young generations who have not learned the conservative values of the past have boldly demanded changes to society's prejudices. That young idol stars and artists can now speak of peace and love is a triumph brought about by such change. K-style is like the total amount of positive energy that Korea possesses.

## On the development and popularity of Korean-style tattoos

In Korea, big tattoos have historically been recognized as a sign of organized crime, because criminals used tattoos to cover up their gang marks. Tattoos were also used to intimidate others, so strong expression and large size were common. In order to break that negative perception and attract non-gang clients, Korean tattooists needed to create a distinctively new style. So we focused on delicate drawing and unique expression. As tattooists started to make a good living, tattooing attracted many talented design, art and craft students, who are abundant and low-paid in Korea.

People's attitudes towards tattoos are very different in Korea across generations. The older generation either had a prejudice towards tattoos or little interest in them, which meant little chance to change their perception. But on social media, prejudice, unfairness and suppression are considered uncool. If something is criticized as such, young people quickly shift their attitude.

The popularity of tattoos among Korean celebrities had a positive impact on removing old prejudices. Young Koreans started to perceive them as cool. Many foreign clients also flew to my studio in Seoul because I tattooed Korean stars they adored. It became part of Hollywood stars' itinerary to get a tattoo while on a promotional tour to South Korea. Just ten years ago, brands didn't want anything to do with tattoos. Now, the dangerous boundaries of tattoo culture make the brand hip by association.

## On his start in tattooing, and his career now

In the 1980s, the government thought that good design could support Korea's export, so Korea now produces the largest number of design graduates in the world. But because there are so many, we barely command minimum wage. I was so angry that my talent wasn't appreciated and looked for another job I could excel at. I chose tattooing. I kept a day job for the first several years, because as a husband and father I couldn't risk the impact doing illegal work could have on my family. But as I became better known, I started tattooing full-time in 2013.

Our clients used to be mostly young women, but we are now getting lots of mothers who want identical tattoos with their daughters. They are so surprised when they see their daughter's tattoo because it is nothing like what they imagined. While in the past, tattoos were a statement to express your identity, now they have become so popular that people perceive them as merely fun fashion.

## On the tattooists' union he is leading

Even though Korean tattooists enjoy global fame and are often invited to work at the best studios in New York or in Paris, back in Korea we live in fear of losing our jobs or jail. While artists are considered difficult to mobilize as a group, we gathered instantly because we had a common goal. Our tattoo union is lobbying lawmakers and providing benefits such as health check-ups, insurance and hygiene education. I also learned that the Korean union group the tattoo union belongs to needed a comprehensive identity for better engagement with the public. So I volunteered to lead the rebranding efforts.

instagram @tattooist_doy

# Lim Kim

Musician and former K-pop idol Yelim Kim

## On her style and influences

The artist Nam June Paik brought a distinctive perspective on Korean culture by mixing memories from his childhood in Korea with his overseas experience. Choi Seung-hee, a legendary dancer in the 1930s, reinterpreted traditional Korean dancing in a contemporary way. While she took her concepts from popular traditional folk dances or Shamanism, she stood out in her time by remixing them with something contemporary. She inspired how I perform and express myself.

I like complexity within simplicity. I choose strong silhouettes and colours when I dress. Music itself can have different colours, like red or purple. Colour adds a distinctive power on the stage and in music videos.

When logic and intuition are balanced, it brings gratifying results. While intuition used to be stronger in me, with my *Generasian* album (2019) logic took an increasingly big role. Making that album involved clear thinking and internalizing what I had learned.

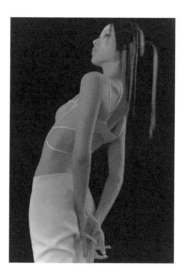

## On living and working in Seoul

Seoul works really hard. I happen to be diligent, and Seoul keeps me moving forward and making new things. Its fast tempo and speed encourage me to keep thinking about my work and push me to achieve the best I can. The process of making my album would have been quite different if I had lived in a more relaxed city. Seoul is melted into my album.

## On the rise of K-style

The rise of pop culture's status and the growth of social media platforms had a major impact. Expressing oneself became more natural. Even though it's still insufficient, society now encourages you to speak up and have a different voice. Through big political moments, strong collective demands were heard. Such chaos and change seem to have brought out a certain style.

I believe K-style is about expressing one's voice, and it is constantly evolving. Korea embraces new things and mixes them. Whether it's natural or not, correct or not, we remix and make it work, which isn't common across Asia.

I've learned that Shamanism is one of the strong bases of Korean culture. We are full of spirit and love singing and dancing. 'Fusion' is a keyword of Korean Shamanism — for instance, there is a strange fusion of Christianity here. K-pop is also a fusion of all genres.

## On leaving her K-pop agency to become independent

Working with an entertainment label, I couldn't push forward my views, and the label wanted me to follow the typical route set out for a female singer in Korea. They insisted the song I hated had to be the title track of my album, and demanded a physical image that I didn't feel comfortable with. I left because I realized that I could only materialize my unlimited potential by leading my own way.

The K-pop industry's size is growing with global influence, but I see little change and improvement from the inside. The system has become more organized, but there isn't much diversity yet. Some might argue that people don't have diverse tastes, but the industry might be hindering musicians across a different or broader spectrum from emerging. Having more character and someone like myself expressing themselves differently might help expand K-style.

## On her working process

After choosing a theme, I conceive a framework for the story and decide how to express my character and voice to tell that story. Then I fill in specific musical components. I constantly ask myself if I'm confident in the story I chose, if it truly expresses what I want, and I'll do research to support it. It was a painful process to do everything on my own to create *Generasian*, but you can only find your own way by many trials and errors.

## On writing a song, 'Yellow', about breaking free of prejudice against Asian women

When I was preparing to debut as Lim Kim, I played some music with a house influence that I was working on to someone big in the music scene in London, and he said, 'That's pretty good, but what's your Korean music like?' It sparked my curiosity towards Korea and Asia. Digging into the topic reminded me of how I've felt confused living as a woman and an Asian.

I thought it would be interesting to express what's really 'oriental' as an Asian, different from Asian appropriation. Since Seoul is westernized, there aren't many opportunities to find meaning in Korean and Eastern culture. That experience enabled me to turn everything upside down and reconsider what is natural. I've also noticed there are very few female Asian musicians in the market.

## On a new movement of independent women in Korea

'I felt stronger and more assertive,' say lots of my fans. Women who often couldn't talk about what made them uncomfortable seemed to feel empowered by me.

Many have suggested that my look needs to be tough to match my songs, with their strong messages, but I didn't change because it didn't feel natural to me. I look calm and quiet. I don't look like someone who will swear. And it brings a twist when I say something aggressive. A fragile-looking young woman can also have a strong voice inside her. I think these women feel encouraged seeing me.

## On future plans

With my first album, I developed a character breaking free of prejudice. I'm delving into how to come up with a new identity in another space, such as video games or virtual reality, and how to illustrate it in an unexpected way. I have come to understand that I have many characters inside me. I pick and pull out a specific identity depending on what I want to express.

instagram @limkim12121

'Koreans are remixing everything cool with no inhibition. In the current world where boundaries between original and copying are so blurry, K-style can appeal globally.'

— Sebastien Falletti, China/East Asia correspondent, *Le Figaro*

CREATIVE ENVIRONMENTS

1MIL
DANCE S
SEO
+82 2 51
STUDIO@1MILLI

CREATIVE ENVIRONMENTS

CREATIVE ENVIRONMENTS

CREATIVE ENVIRONMENTS

CREATIVE ENVIRONMENTS

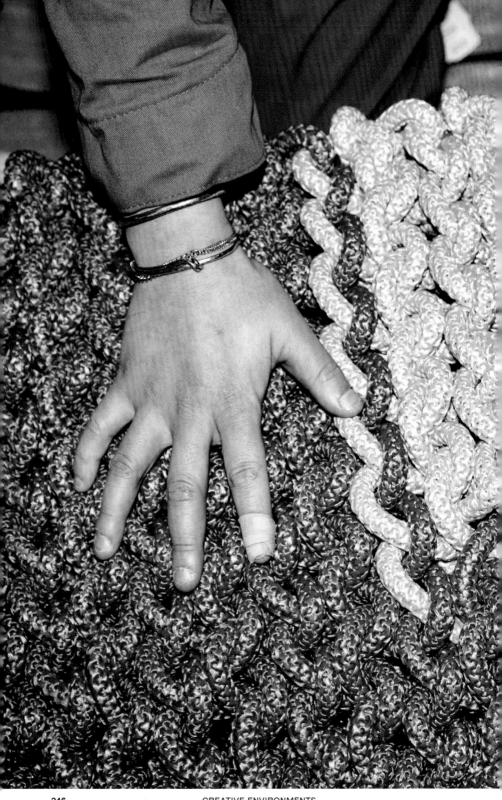

CREATIVE ENVIRONMENTS

CREATIVE ENVIRONMENTS

CREATIVE ENVIRONMENTS

CREATIVE ENVIRONMENTS

패턴 원피스

메쉬탑

카모 스커트

베

블레이저

파자마팬츠

사커저지

슬리브리스

가죽 베스트

버튼업 셔츠

막이

CREATIVE ENVIRONMENTS

CREATIVE ENVIRONMENTS

CREATIVE ENVIRONMENTS

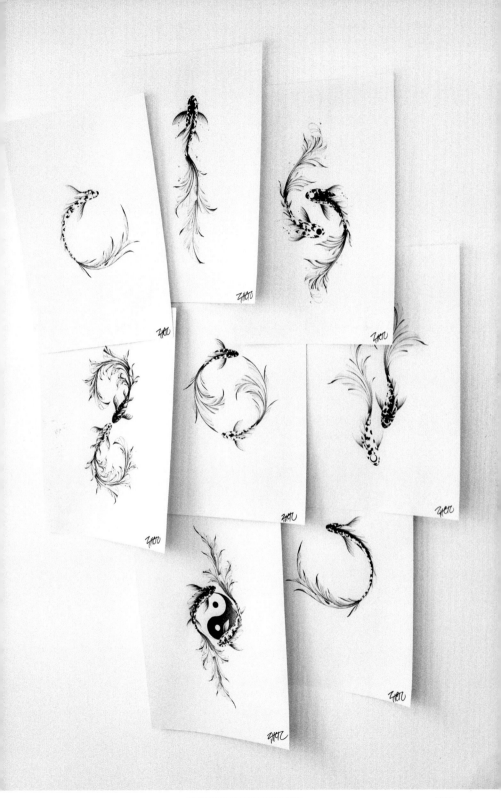

CREATIVE ENVIRONMENTS

CREATIVE ENVIRONMENTS

CREATIVE ENVIRONMENTS

# Danny Chung

Danny Chung is a songwriter and A&R at
THEBLACKLABEL, and has been involved behind the
scenes of many K-pop hits for nearly a decade.

## On the evolution and future of K-pop

What really put a battery in my back to even attempt being an artist or songwriter myself was seeing acts like 1TYM and Drunken Tiger. These artists showed me what it looked like when a Korean kid like myself gets on stage and performs.

The second generation of K-pop tried to bring K-pop to Western audiences by featuring Western artists and Korean artists that didn't necessarily make sense. It underestimated the intelligence and connections that fans had, and it felt contrived, not genuine. It watered down what K-pop was supposed to be at that moment.

After failed attempts at global crossover, Korea went back to its original roots. Labels became more insular and focused on making music for Korea. Global takeover wasn't the plan, but the audiences came back because they recognized how genuine and authentic it felt. I started getting personally involved in the industry in 2014, working with YG Entertainment. The moment that K-pop was having was unprecedented and my gut feeling was that it would be fleeting. I was very wrong.

K-pop's influence has far outgrown the peninsula of Korea itself. The culture has touched every corner of the globe, and through social media, conversations are being had that weren't possible before. The first generation of K-pop came to be far before social media existed and maybe even before the internet itself. I lived in Philadelphia, and the Korean community there was not big at all. The only way to consume Korean pop culture was to physically get yourself to one of the two Korean video rental shops or the one Korean music store in town. Now algorithms have every individual figured out and literally throw K-pop content in your face if you're even slightly interested in the culture, which I think is a great thing. Access is invaluable and it's being given out freely. Early Korean pop culture was cultivated specifically for the Korean audience, not because it was being gatekept, but because there was just no way to get it to the mass market, and equally, the mass market was not interested. As K-pop evolved, the audience evolved alongside it. Now that it is a global phenomenon, the content has the responsibility of being aware of its global influence.

People around me have these conversations all the time. We want to spread a positive message. At the end of the day, we are just trying to make people dance and sing. There has been a more active effort to westernize and globalize K-pop. And now, we actually have the resources and partnerships to do that because the US labels understand it is a real force. There is a real core fandom with a deep burning passion. K-pop is moving to become a bit more Western, but it's being done in a much more organic and authentic way. I didn't see anybody like me who got anywhere in terms of success in music. Now for little Korean boys and girls in America, it's normal to see Korean bands on late-night shows. There are no limits for them.

## On the relationship between the mainstream and street or subculture

Street culture dictates what mainstream culture will be...even the biggest acts in K-pop that I'm around are in tune with what's happening in the subcultures of Seoul. The stars that live in Cheongdam and Hannam are friends or at least in close proximity to the fashionable street kids in Itaewon and Hongdae, and are inspired by their creativity and tenacious approach to being different. Being different is precious, especially in a collectivist society such as Korea that has historically been homogenous in culture and mindset. The younger generation consciously takes action to break these moulds and create a new narrative. Cakeshop is a club in Itaewon that was an incubator of culture where K-pop and street culture overlapped. A few years ago, on any given night, you could see G-Dragon or CL and their crew partying with the Itaewon street kids that were really shaping the culture from the ground up.

## On K-pop and fashion

Many notable idols are known to have an 'effect', where any product they're seen with (from potato chips to paper towels) will fly off the shelves. These idols are walking billboards in the best, most valuable way possible. When G-Dragon was seen stepping on the back heels of his Vans, wearing them like slippers, it became a viral fashion trend and eventually Vans made an official version. I experienced a bit of this effect first-hand. Before doing songwriting with YG,

I was making music independently. In one of my music videos, I wore a vintage Seoul '88 Olympics cap. My former manager, who was managing G-Dragon, showed him the video. G-Dragon and Taeyang decided to wear that specific cap in their 'Good Boy' video. After the video was released, bootleg versions of that hat were being made and sold worldwide. You couldn't walk down the street without seeing a fake version of it. You could look on eBay right now and still find that hat being sold. It amazes me that a simple fashion choice I made for a no-budget music video had such a lasting impact on the general population globally through the power of K-pop.

## On Korean Americans in K-pop

There are many artists in Korean music who were raised in America and wanted to chase their dreams there, but America did not have a clue how to market Asian artists and didn't want to take a chance. These artists made an exodus to Korea. More and more major American record labels sign K-pop acts and cause serious disruption on the Billboard charts. I had to leave my home country because it would not recognize me, and ironically, it was me leaving and working in Korea that showed America how valuable I could be.

instagram @thedannychung

# Elaine YJ Lee

Contributor to *i-D*, *Highsnobiety*, *SSENSE*, *Apartamento*, *Document Journal* and more, with a focus on fashion and Korean culture. Former Managing Editor of *HYPEBEAST* Korea.

## On her brief stint in K-pop styling

When I moved back to Seoul from New York in 2015–16, I got the opportunity to work under stylist Ji Eun at YG Entertainment. I had grown up immersed in K-pop since elementary school, and was obsessed with it more for its fashion than the music itself. I dare say that Ji Eun should be credited for revolutionizing the look of K-pop through Big Bang. While K-pop is now lauded for its impeccable, innovative style thanks to global acts like BTS and Blackpink, in the early to mid-2010s, much of K-pop fashion was still dominated by matchy-matchy, costumey looks (think schoolgirl/boy uniforms, or tonal looks where each band member just wore different colours). That still exists today, but I think Big Bang really gave K-pop style a complete facelift. They are the ones that truly started to mix high and low fashion, both from abroad and from cultural elements unique to Korea.

Immediately, I was shocked at the gruelling schedule of K-pop styling, and the amount of physical work it required. We would go over a week without sleep, and joke that the only time we could eat or sleep was when we were on an airplane, travelling on tour. The work that goes on behind the scenes for a seemingly glamorous result is not so glamorous at all. Despite this, I could never forget the energy and synergy I felt when I saw the artists and dancers on stage wearing the clothes that I had helped put together. That momentary excitement is incomparable to being at an ordinary fashion shoot. The few months I spent at YG were an exhilarating adrenaline rush.

## On changes in Korea's digital fashion sector

It's only been about five years, but it's hard to imagine Korea without a platform like *HYPEBEAST* now. It just makes so much sense for a market like Korea. In the initial stages of the launch, when looking at local competitors — in terms of magazines and online publications — there really wasn't a comparable local platform, with similar speed in news delivery and scale. We had to work hard to establish our presence there; I was shocked when a senior person at a large sportswear label hadn't heard about the media brand. It was also difficult to find writers who were well-versed in the global language of street culture and immersed in Seoul's local scene at the same time. Few editors with tenure at bigger, more traditional publications could adapt to the speed and new way of publishing content online. Naturally, new media needs new, young, more web-savvy storytellers.

We had an aggressive growth strategy where we posted at least one article an hour on the website and social media. At first, we would get feedback from people who thought it was too much, too frequent. Now, it's the norm. I believe *HYPEBEAST* Korea established the system of talking about fashion products and news releases very quickly in the region. In a year, we were the fastest-growing *HYPEBEAST* platform out of all of the media brand's other language versions. I credit not only our hard work, but also the readiness of the market. There was, and still is, an insatiable demand to consume digital fashion content constantly, because Koreans are online more than anyone, more than ever.

## On choosing which brands to cover

Part of the process of filtering through the hundreds of press releases I used to receive every day was to look into each brand's affiliations. Were they respected and consumed by those who are respected in the industry? Who are their friends? Who has worn them? I'd check their background and community. This also meant looking at their educational and professional history: in the case of a fashion brand, did the founder or designer go to a prestigious school like Central Saint Martins? Or do they have experience designing at a famous, luxury brand? But over the course of a few years, this changed. While many successful brand founders used to study or work abroad in places like London and New York, I noticed a rise in the relevance of brands and individuals who were wholly formed in Korea. There is an increasing number of creative imprints paving their own path and original identity in Korea. You don't need to reach or look too far beyond the country's borders for inspiration any more.

## On the evolving diversity of Korea's modelling industry

In 2015, I wrote a feature for *Highsnobiety* diving into the different factors that lead Asian brands to hire white models. The story extended beyond Korea to Asia more broadly, including Japan, Singapore and India. The gist of it was that many Asian brands try to establish a sense of history to build credibility, and this was a major reason they hired white models. Since much of pop culture is perceived as coming from the West, and Asian brands are relatively newer than Western ones, having white models gave them the illusion of having a certain history.

It also had to do with the brands' ambition to sell globally. One Korean brand felt that it needed to hire a white model to sell in the UK. At the time of writing the article, the global modelling industry was dominated by white models, and Asian brands followed because they needed to be competitive in that market. When they hired Black models, it would be to borrow from Black culture such as hip-hop.

I think that's still very prevalent, but with some improvements. Since then, there have been plenty of local brands that are innovative and relevant and use models from diverse backgrounds. This shift in recent years highlights the fact that the Korean fashion industry is on its way to understanding its own identity and position, and what it means to be a global citizen.

instagram @elaineyjlee

# Jason Schlabach

Jason Schlabach is a brand builder and creator of **RYSE** Hotel
in Hongdae, Seoul. He is passionate about subcultures and the artistic
expressions found within.

## On first impressions of Korean style

I was struck by how Koreans are very open about what it takes to achieve their style. There is something honest about that approach, which is cool. Take the example of beauty and grooming regimes – in a place like the US, I'd say the prevailing trend is to pretend it's all natural and effortless. In Korea, when you're sharing a mirror with someone before they head into the office or somewhere public, you see all the work that goes into being presentable (and these are guys!). They don't pretend they always look this way. 'Yes, I do try. I'm working hard at my style.' I think it's so refreshing that there is equal pride in the process as much as the result.

## On the defining elements of K-style

Communality is still important. 'Twinning' trends are not as strong as four or five years ago, but what lay underneath that trend was a communal way of creating style tribes, which is still there. K-style is not especially individualistic. It means developing your own style along with your group of friends, in a shared experience.

I've noticed in Korea that young people's identity and style are more self-constructed than inherited through upbringing and family. The relatively recent economic boom of Korea is likely responsible for that. In the West, parents influence their kids' relationship to style. For instance, you might inherit a car brand affiliation. Your family is a Ford family or a Dodge family, possibly for three or four generations. You have feelings about the world through the lens of brand and aesthetic choices. All kids rebel, but they have something to set that rebellion against. In Korea there is a real desire to learn about culture, brands and styles from Korea, Asia and worldwide because many young people didn't get that from their parents. Developing the basis of their style becomes a really communal search among friends and peers. When a certain model of sneakers becomes popular in Seoul, you walk out of the subway, and it's like 'Who sent out the message?' Everyone is wearing the same sneakers.

## On the rise of K-style

The recent changes in Korean style and influence were visible throughout Asia. Living initially in Hong Kong and then spending long periods in Korea and Singapore has shown me how rapid and powerful that influence was. I used to be able to walk down the street in Hong Kong and spot the visiting Korean travellers immediately by their style. Hairstyles, beauty trends and Korean fashion labels made them stand out, and I could see many people take notice. Gradually, I began to find it more difficult to identify who was from Korea and who had adopted the styles they saw in K-pop, K-dramas and in streetstyle blogs. Now, the greater availability of e-commerce has resulted in style signatures from Seoul reaching across Asia and worldwide. It's really common to see Hangul characters on T-shirts in Singapore, idol haircuts in Shanghai, Ader Error fashion on Berlin gallery staff at Art Basel.

## On living and working in Seoul

Seoul was not a city that I understood quickly or at once, and that made it really fascinating for me. There is a depth of knowledge and history within the arts and graphic design that adds a lot of complexity to the current styles. And that's juxtaposed with big swathes of the city that are 'undesigned' in a way that's hard to find elsewhere in our hyper-aesthetic world. I'm talking about the amazing yellow crates from the markets that form temporary art installations on the sidewalks every night; the ubiquitous roll-down garage doors with yellow, blue, red stripes; the metal chopsticks that are universal across a certain price point of restaurant; and so many other utilitarian and strangely compelling designs. I borrowed, stole and improvised with many of those techniques and materials at RYSE. The key was to meld 'high' design with functional materials and elements that are often overlooked and covered in the final stage of a spatial or graphic design. It inspired me to bring raw concrete, risograph prints that highlight imperfection, sculptures composed of construction steel, a 1930s vinyl lathe, painted plywood art installations and other utilitarian elements into a hotel experience that has to be comfortable, luxurious and uplifting for guests.

The fast-fashion, music-video, trend-driven elements of Korean style were not what I was interested in. The aspects that appealed to the RYSE brand and were incorporated were how to mix and match, and to combine really unexpected references.

## On Seoul's eye-catching street style

I was inspired by how studied and careful many of the outfit choices were for the youth, especially in coordination with each other. For a time in 2017, 'twinning' or wearing the same tee, shoes or jacket among a friendship group was everywhere to be seen. I wanted RYSE to become a destination for that type of night out among friends. Not exclusive and out of reach, but really stylish and equally iconic to the looks they were trying to pull off.

During the construction of the hotel, I constantly saw examples of how the commonplace was casually, sometimes unintentionally stylish in Korea. The plumbing and structural elements of the construction were incredibly colourful and bright, and created vignettes of surprising beauty. Even the construction workers had style in their functional gear, from camouflage neckwarmers in the winter to mesh panelling in their tops in the summer.

## On music and subculture

I saw Korean cultural tribes as having really strong social connections. 360 Sounds is a group of DJs and musicians that has had a huge role in the spreading of great music throughout Seoul and Korea. The mixture of respect, genuine friendship and loyalty that I saw among the crew stays with me today. They have stayed true to the music and their mission to bring it directly to the audience night after night in clubs, mixes and their own music. The longevity of the group and addition of newer members as they go along mean they're always evolving, but never trend-driven.

instagram @jasonschlabach

**Sukwoo Hong (a.k.a. Your Boyhood)**

Korean Fashion Directory

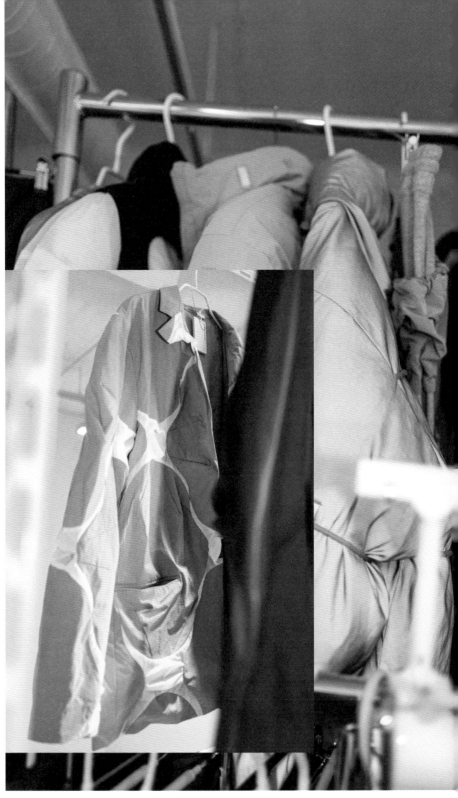

# PAF
# (Post Archive
# Faction)

What does 'Post Archive Faction' mean? Officially, its brand director and founder Dongjoon Lim explains that the diverse cultures and people who exist between the history of numerous 'archives', and the process of building 'post and next generation archives' made the brand name. Unofficially, Lim grew up under his father, who was a devoted activist fighting for democracy in the 1980s. The existence of a political party seeking different values immensely influenced his perspective on the world. Instead of accepting existing information as it is, he has questions. What is really right? PAF gives 'Left, Centre, Right' labels to all the clothing in each of its collections.

For every PAF collection, there is a 'Right, Fundamental Model', which can be worn by a relatively large number of people, a 'Left, Radical Model', the most advanced model that layers research on modelling and ergonomics, and a 'Centre, Bridging Model' which mixes values of both.

A T-shirt that considers commerciality and high-end ready-to-wear pieces that show the brand's philosophy coexist in one collection. Lim has said that this expresses PAF's 'factional' brand identity, but it is also how a small fashion label survives. He has consistently maintained this principle since 2017, when he first planned the brand, and has since built PAF into one of the most experimental and intriguing fashion labels.

Unlike many designers, before creating PAF, Lim was not immersed in fashion. Instead, his greatest pleasure as a teenager was to figure out the structure of a new object that did not exist in the manual and assemble it himself. The biggest reason for his choice to major in industrial design at university was his teenage dedication to assembling LEGO. Seeing him in a calm, black Comme des Garçons jacket and trousers, one might feel he is a bit out of place as the creative director of an avant-garde fashion label. He studied fashion first, rather than enjoyed it. After following thousands of fashion brands' Facebook pages, he observed how they made collections, showcased clothes and created campaigns.

Creating the actual shape of the clothes he envisioned was only possible because of his work with co-founder and expert modellist Sookyo Jeong. Turning a small house in Bogwang-dong, Itaewon, into their studio, the two prepared for the brand's first collection. This included various methods of using tightening drawstrings, creating down jackets, sweatpants and coats that were dismantled and recombined from the basic structure

KOREAN FASHION DIRECTORY

of clothing on a virtual 'runway' stage. After all the photos of the collection were taken, the runway set, built somewhere in Gyeonggi-do, was burned. Lim recorded the whole process on video, as 'a kind of declaration that marked the start of the PAF'.

When he first started PAF, Lim thought that anonymity and statelessness were necessary to express the brand's identity. This approach has sparked curiosity among consumers around the world. Lim does not show his process of inspiration or a narrative for his collections. Almost all PAF collections feature male models with mostly covered faces, who don't try to express any kind of lifestyle. Instead of talking about the fantasy of fashion, he describes his approach as simply choosing a method that shows the typical details, silhouettes and characteristics of PAF. For him, fashion is a reality, a history of records that he faithfully builds.

While filming their brand campaign for 2021, some of these preoccupations were dropped. Lim showed a photo of a model wearing the PAF 4.0 collection that appears to be infinitely proliferating, against a backdrop of a beach in a small Korean town. 'For some reason, I thought this photo was very "Korean". In my early twenties, I had strong negative thoughts about "Seoul" and "Korea". I thought that if it had been a different city, it could have been more popular. But I have changed my mind a bit. I don't think there is any other place more fun than Seoul. I began to love Seoul more.'

Today, PAF Studio, located in a residential area a little way from downtown Seoul, is busy as usual. Creating new patterns and preparing for various collaborations, its crew members are constantly having conversations while doing their own work. Before starting this interview, Lim introduced me to the members of the PAF one by one. To him, PAF is not a 'fashion brand'. Although clothes play a big role, I imagine him eventually expanding slowly into all the categories he has influenced and documented, such as art, industrial design and architecture. This is why the brand name is 'Post Archive Faction', not 'Dongjoon Lim'.

postarchivefaction.com
instagram @postarchivefaction

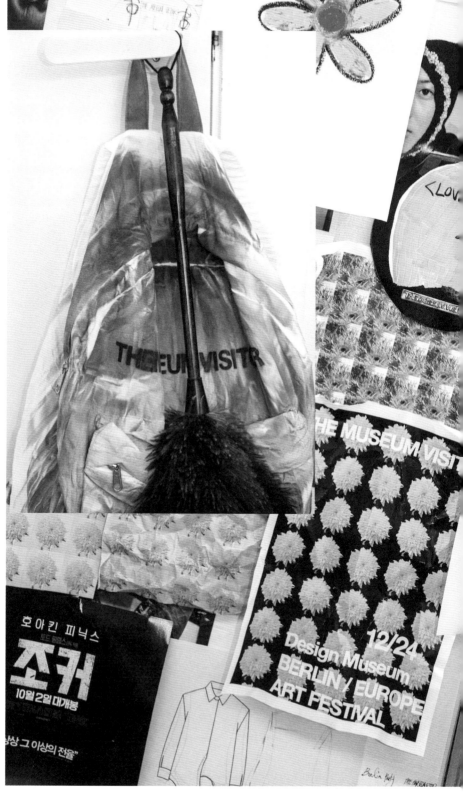

# THE MUSEUM VISITOR

The Museum Visitor embodies memories of San Francisco and Berlin, where its founder Moonsu Park spent his daily life focusing on drawing and visiting galleries. I first encountered his work in 2018, in a collection made up of clothes that combined tailoring techniques and the creator's (somewhat private) thoughts. For a designer, Park's way and flow of expressing ideas are not typical. In his collections, the debate as to whether to go with something 'current' or classic is evident. The work presented in his show in 2018 broadly overlapped with the conversations I had with him, as well as his attitudes and the tastes seen throughout his studio, displaying an uncommonly clear sense of style.

It's not difficult to make a brand in Korea. The country's largest fashion e-commerce platform, MUSINA, has more than 3,000 local brands. Streetwear, which has gained a stronger influence over the years, still prevails. Certain brands are not so different from fast fashion. The Museum Visitor's work feels fresh because even though Park is a young designer, he does not seek to reflect popular, current trends. A man wandering around Seoul wearing old Levi's 501 jeans, well-made leather shoes and a classic watch, in a white shirt with finely cut yet experimental details: this is the image evoked by The Museum Visitor.

The Museum Visitor continues to expand into new realms, with bigger stores, a broader range of customers and friends who understand his ideas. It's interesting that Park did not mean to start a fashion brand in the beginning. While he has been interested in clothes since his school days, he never thought he would become a fashion designer. Instead, he was deeply into paintings. Flowers and houses, which filled up the white canvas from the natural stroke of brushes, intense abstract expressions and a few words are all features that have slowly appeared at the forefront of his collections.

People are not looking for merely 'style' in The Museum Visitor's collections. Traces of hand-finished paint mark the hooded parka that fits the body well, and the trompe-l'oeil trench coat. This brand's fans wear something because of their connection with its artistic perspective. One famous Korean actor purchased an item out of stock simply by sending a direct message to Park. In this way, a little-known brand has become something instantly recognizable by Koreans who enjoy fashion.

In the summer of 2021, Park looked at the path along which his brand had grown. There are certain differences between the early collections, which incorporated the word 'atelier', and the current collection. Although he made clothing for men from the beginning, a large number of his customers were women. In autumn 2021, he officially launched a women's collection. A windbreaker in see-through material and wide-hemmed trousers with a little silkscreen patchwork that reads 'BERLIN, PARIS, SEOUL' are displayed at the store along with a hand-drawn doormat showing flowers and a smile. Gender isn't so important to The Museum Visitor's collection.

Park often uses the words 'avant-garde', 'art love' and 'rock' in reference to his brand. When someone uses these words on their clothing, it usually diminishes my interest in the brand, because their meanings feel too obvious. But when I come across them in The Museum Visitor's collection, and talk to Park in person, it's easy to fall for him and his brand. The Museum Visitor's collection and its founder's thoughts smoothly coincide.

the--museum--visitor.com
instagram @themuseumvisitor

# After Pray

I met After Pray in 2018, a little while before they launched their first runway collection for Spring/Summer 2019 at Seoul Fashion Week. Two young men in their early twenties, Sungvin Jo and Injun Park decided to launch a brand together because they loved similar fashion designers. They decided on a brand name and then continued their studies for several years, focusing on menswear, patterns and clothes-making practices in Paris and Seoul respectively. This brand, which mixes the atmosphere and graphics of streetwear, the practical materials and patterns of sportswear and the sensibility of high-end ready-to-wear, did not just pop out of nowhere.

'Based on a collection that evokes the imagination of "the youth of the dynamic city of the future", we aim to become a brand where the elements of modern menswear are delicately changed', says Jo, 'because I like it. That's what we're trying to put [in the brand].' Its two founders do not define After Pray as a single genre; if one could describe it in one word, it would be hybrid. They combine tailoring, military looks, a streetwear sensibility and practical elements of workwear and sportswear to create their look. 'We are trying to design more sophisticated and reasonable products that are in line with today's trends,' says Jo. After Pray's design language reconstructs a broad cultural foundation, with elements extracted from different fields such as art, literature and subculture into contemporary, witty collections. Its founders coordinate the entire process of preparing, completing and presenting the collections. Much has changed from the time when designers could simply present collections twice a year and wait for customers to visit stores in person; now, Korean fashion brands have to constantly present various works in order to communicate directly with their customers as a brand, in addition to simply making clothes.

Park talks about the need to communicate with a wider audience while thinking about sales: 'In the past, designing, knitting patterns and making clothes were all in my head. There is so much to think about now, but one learns a lot as well...like how to communicate, what kind of content to create and show.' On After Pray's official Instagram account you'll find serious campaign images alongside sometimes light-hearted or curious images, with no elaborate explanations. Boys are walking the streets wearing After Pray, opening invitations against the backdrop of a flower garden, taking selfies at home and talking with their friends.

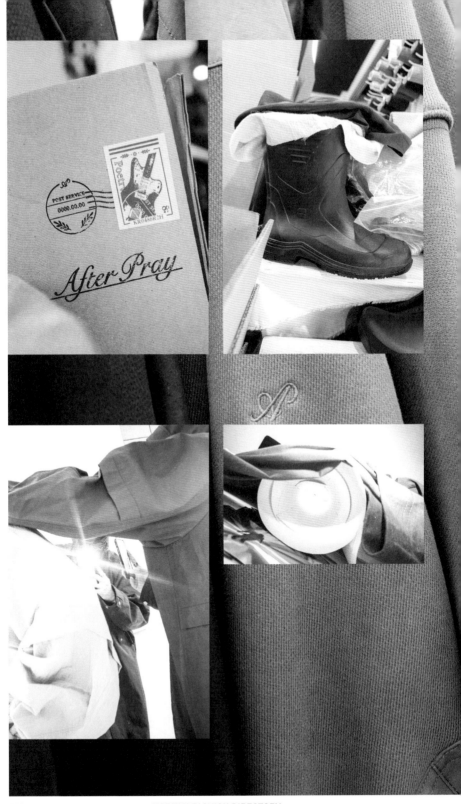

In 2021, having just finished the presentation of their eighth collection, they moved from Hannam-dong to Sinseol-dong. Leaving a showroom that had been in operation for over a year, they decided to move to a much larger space to use as a studio. 'Personally, I am moving ahead in a better direction than I imagined. I have been aiming for a brand with more character. As we enter our fourth year, it allows us to look at our brand from a distance. We're doing modern fashion while revealing our colours, so I thought this route was okay,' says Jo of their move. The road they have taken to create a menswear brand since they were young — a serious goal rather than a simple wish - differentiates After Pray from other young fashion brands.

The showroom business is also preparing for a full-fledged overseas expansion. 'We plan to reach out to more diverse people. While marketing boldly, it is a priority to focus on our solid ground. Now that we have a domestic sales network, we want to challenge the foreign market. We will make people imagine our vision in a variety of ways and incorporate a forward-looking attitude', says Park.

After Pray is careful and serious in some ways. But like many modern fashion brands, it knows how to improvise and collaborate. The unique vision of two boys who like clothes above all else has slowly permeated their brand.

afterpray.com
instagram @afterpray_official

# DOCUMENT

Jongsoo Lee has been in the fashion industry since 2001. While working as a designer for other brands, including a corporate ready-to-wear label often dubbed a 'national brand', he always dreamed of creating his own. DOCUMENT started from the personal archives he worked on and collected for over ten years. Since Spring/Summer 2015, when he unveiled his first collection, he has been weaving 'repetition and difference', inspired by the French philosopher Gilles Deleuze's early work *Différence et Répétition* (1968), which forms the most important basis for his brand. Instead of the general concept of a new season, DOCUMENT's collection has been built up by overlapping repetitions. Lee says, 'The process of accumulating repeated experiences has its own uniqueness and becomes a precious memory for individuals. When I was preparing for the brand in earnest around 2013, I locked myself away for six months looking at photos and materials. Looking back, I felt that I had changed a lot. Naturally, I came to the thought, "What hasn't changed?" Then, when I opened the wardrobe, there were only navy and white colours. I thought, "This is it." In it, there were always repetitions, differences, and repetitions of differences.' For him, repetition and difference were, after all, an approach to 'life': 'Everyday life repeats itself, but there are bound to be differences, and people are inevitably different despite the countless repetitions to make up for them.'

In a pure white studio in an alley of the factory district in Seongsu-dong — the same place where the first collection began in 2015, where the surroundings have since begun to alter bit by bit — the changed and the unchanged coexist. The 'DOCUMENT CX Store' on the first floor of the building, facing the studio, is the biggest change. In a small, white store, a collection that fully reflects the brand's identity, from finely tailored jackets to relaxed navy blue wool coats, is ready to welcome customers. There are also camel coats, jeans made of stiff Japanese Hickory denim, knitted piqué tops and shirts that appear to be one colour at first glance, but are in fact subtly different.

Like a paint palette with slight differences in colour saturation and lightness, the clothes, in tones around and beyond indigo and white, slowly reveal subtle differences in their build quality and materials. DOCUMENT clothes don't possess the immediate visual delight of youth fashions that have recently swept the streets. Instead, their appeal is revealed gradually, over

time. Like hand–stamps and labels on clothes that can be cut and collected, another feature of DOCUMENT, the feeling of being touched by people's hands despite being ready–to–wear, is evident throughout the store.

After completing his fourteenth collection, Lee began to ask 'Where am I now?' The preceding eight years had been a path towards making clothes and building a brand, as well as contemplating maintenance and sustainability. Although 'growth' was an objective from the beginning, he had started with the central idea that he should begin with as little as possible and maintain it. 'The reality…was not as rosy as expected. I continued to ponder, "Should DOCUMENT hit a limit at some point, shall I launch a new [better selling] brand?"' Instead, DOCUMENT knocked on the door of the foreign market. It is now stocked in leading stores in the US, France, Italy and Germany, China, Thailand and Japan. Lee saw that Korean fashion was riding a current to some extent: 'There has been a trend in the Korean menswear market in recent years to support small independent Korean brands, which are the opposite of people flocking to the glamorous side of foreign Fashion Week collections.' Just as continental hegemony shifted to the US from Europe from the eighteenth to the twenty–first centuries, he speculates that it might come to Asia. 'Looking at Korea, sandwiched between Japan, which has dominated [fashion], and gigantic China, the "Korean Wave" seems to be a sign that eventually, it is going to grow evenly. Should I call it a sense of duty? I want to influence the dreams of young folks who are studying fashion design now. I want them to see that I did it, so they can do it someday.'

Subtle changes that appear little by little, the mechanisms of repetition and difference, are present in DOCUMENT's collection. The clothing looks at first like a single mass, but as you get closer, the texture emerges, and the closer you look, the more detail you see. And when you put on the clothes, hidden elements are revealed. To Lee, 'approaching strongly' is the feeling you give when you keep piling up small things. Rather than presenting a new object, it is as if the accumulation of stacking tens of thousands of small matchsticks is released. Although it looks ordinary at first, through the accumulation of time, it has tremendous weight. Such a notion seems unlikely to change for DOCUMENT.

document-document.com
instagram @_document

# Seoul Map

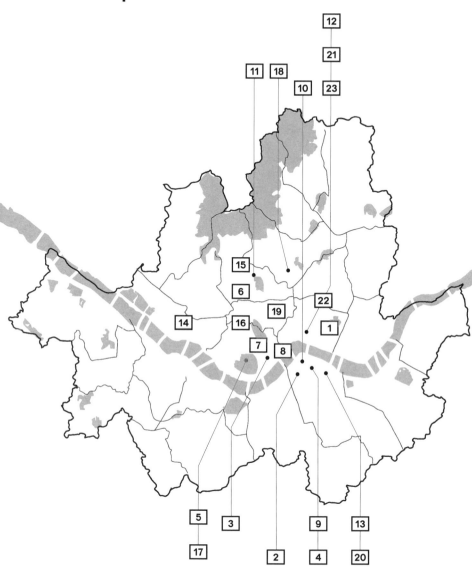

| | | |
|---|---|---|
| 1 | **Lia Kim**<br>**25–29** | 33, Ttukseom–ro 13–gil, Seongdong–gu<br>성동구 뚝섬로 13길 33 원밀리언 댄스 스튜디오 |
| 2 | **Youngjin Kim**<br>**30–34** | Eonju–ro, Gangnam–gu<br>강남구 신사동 |
| 3 | **DPR REM**<br>**35–40** | Itaewon–ro, Yongsan–gu<br>용산구 한남동 |

| 4 | **Xu Meen** <br> **73–76** | Apgujeong-ro, Gangnam-gu <br> 강남구 압구정로 |
|---|---|---|
| 5 | **Serian Heu** <br> **77–81** | Hybe, 42 Hangang-daero, Yongsan-gu <br> 하이브, 용산구 한강대로 42 |
| 6 | **BAJOWOO** <br> **82–84** | 6F, 35, Myeongdong 4-gil, Jung-gu <br> 중구 명동2가 53-9 6층 |
| 7 | **IISE** <br> **85–88** | 3F, 210-7, Noksapyeong-daero, Yongsan-gu <br> 용산구 녹사평대로 210-7 3층 |
| 8 | **Nana Youngrong Kim** <br> **121–25** | Jangmun-ro, Yongsan-gu <br> 용산구 한남동 |
| 9 | **Mischief** <br> **126–30** | 3F, 31, Apgujeong-ro 46-gil, Gangnam-gu <br> 강남구 압구정로 46길 31 3층 |
| 10 | **Kyuhee Baik** <br> **131–36** | Stüssy Seoul Chapter, 42, Apgujeong-ro 46 gil, Gangnam-gu <br> 강남구 압구정로46길 42 |
| 11 | **Teo Yang** <br> **169–73** | 97-8, Gyedong-gil, Jongno-gu <br> 종로구 계동길 97-8 태오양스튜디오 |
| 12 | **Kwangho Lee** <br> **174–78** | 12-6, Seongsuil-ro 1-gil, Seongdong-gu <br> 성동구 성수일로 1길 12-6 |
| 13 | **Mingoo Kang** <br> **179–84** | 19, Dosan-daero 67-gil, Gangnam-gu <br> 강남구 도산대로67길 19 |
| 14 | **Hwang Soyoon** <br> **217–21** | 13, Wausan-ro 29-gil, Mapo-gu <br> 마포구 와우산로 29길 13 |
| 15 | **Doy** <br> **222–26** | 2F, 59, Jahamun-ro, Jongno-gu <br> 종로구 자하문로59, 2층 INKEDWALL |
| 16 | **Lim Kim** <br> **227–32** | Huam-dong, Yongsan-gu <br> 용산구 후암동 |
| 17 | **Danny Chung** <br> **265–69** | Itaewon-dong, Yongsan-gu <br> 용산구 이태원동 |
| 18 | **Sukwoo Hong** <br> **280–97** | 6F, 165 Bomun-ro, Seongbuk-gu <br> 성북구 보문로 165, 6층 |
| 19 | **PAF, studio** <br> **282–85** | 71, Dongho-ro 10-gil, Jung-gu <br> 중구 동호로10길 71(신당동), 4층 |
| 20 | **The Museum Visitor** <br> **286–89** | 14, Dosan-daero 67-gil, Gangnam-gu <br> 강남구 도산대로67길 14(청담동) 3층 301호 |
| 21 | **House By, store** <br> **286–89** | 13, Gwangnaru-ro 4ga-gil, Seongdong-gu <br> 성동구 광나루로4가길 13(성수동2가), 1층 |
| 22 | **After Pray** <br> **290–93** | 19, Cheonho-daero 12-gil, Dongdaemun-gu <br> 동대문구 천호대로12길 19(용두동), 401 |
| 23 | **DOCUMENT, store** <br> **294–97** | 27, Seongsuil-ro 12-gil, Seongdong-gu <br> 성동구 성수일로12길 27, B동 1층(성수동2가) |

# Credits

# Acknowledgments

The idea of *Make Break Remix: The Rise of K-style* was born in 2018, when a dear friend, Sarah Ichioka, an urbanist, writer and curator, told Lucas Dietrich, international editorial director at Thames & Hudson, that it was time to produce a book about Korean culture, and introduced us. Although I was very tempted to take on such an exciting project, I lacked the confidence to navigate the unfamiliar world of music and fashion. After several months of attempting to figure out how to make a viable book about ever-changing Korean pop culture, I became a mother and dropped the project. Lucas saved the book by contacting me after a year, asking me to rekindle our dialogue. Having felt deep regret about letting the most fascinating undertaking slip through my fingers, I armed myself with a new conviction that I would shed light on what makes K-style successful and where it is heading.

Interviewing trailblazers who are shaping K-style felt like the best solution, but selecting the right people was a daunting task and took almost a year. Rich Lim, a Korean American branding expert with deep insights, was instrumental in forming a direction. Teo Yang, my trusted former client, also shared his wisdom. It wasn't easy to pick people who garner genuine respect rather than commercial appeal. Rich and Kyuhee Baik helped me to stay focused. Kyuhee also introduced my wonderful partner less_TAEKYUN KIM, who was perfect to illustrate the authentic K-style, with his raw and low-key perspectives and deep understanding of youth culture. Serian Heu kindly recommended a few interviewees. Sukwoo Hong (a.k.a. Your Boyhood), a prominent fashion journalist, provided invaluable advice in the early stage and enriched the book by generously leading the Korean Fashion Directory. There were many people with international recognition, but it was important to select the ones Koreans consider their own. Jason Schlabach, who is well-versed in both Korean and international creative scenes, helped me steer and also recommended Hezin O, our wonderful designer, who created a beautiful book reflecting the spirit of the project.

I cannot thank enough all the nineteen interviewees, including three marvellous commentators, who kindly shared candid and fascinating stories about their work and life in Korea despite their unbelievably hectic schedules. Their generosity and inspiration made the book possible. When I started, there were only four people with whom I had any kind of contact. Amazingly, I secured one after another on my ambitious target list thanks to the mutual respect and admiration among interviewees, and their enthusiasm for what they believed was a fun and meaningful project. I conducted most of the interviews during the first lockdown in London over video calls, and their bursting energy kept me sane and energized.

I'm grateful to Na Kim, percipient interpreter of the creative scene in Korea, who led space design for the 'Hallyu!' exhibition at the V&A, for kindly writing the foreword. Marc Cansier, founding partner of brand master-planner Marc & Chantal, Sebastien Falletti, *Le Figaro*'s China/East Asia correspondent (who spent almost ten years in Korea), Andrew Tuck, Editor-in-Chief of *Monocle* and DJ Soulscape (Min Jun Park), founder of 360 Sounds, provided penetrating quotes on K-style. I also thank Sebastien for many rounds of stimulating discussions throughout the different stages of the book. Choe Sang-hun, *The New York Times*'s long-time correspondent in Korea, whom I admire for his deep comprehension of Korea, and Kim Ji-yeon, one of the two producers who created the dazzling Neflix series *Squid Game*, were so kind to offer recommendations for the book.

Augusta Pownall at Thames & Hudson expertly guided me through my first experience of authoring a book and offered me much-needed encouragement in early days. My brilliant editor Kate Edwards was always there solving problems with me. Both Augusta and Kate made me believe that they genuinely liked the book, which is the best love you can get from your publisher. Gary Hayes, the book's wonderful production controller at Thames & Hudson, looked after the proofing and materials.

I am grateful to my husband George, the harshest critic of the book, who also graciously endured being a single dad for more than fourteen weeks over my multiple trips to Korea (during COVID), our little boy Jun, the sunshine of my life, whom I hope will grow to be as brave and creative as the people in this book, and my parents, who always believed in me.

First published in the United Kingdom in 2022 by
Thames & Hudson Ltd, 181A High Holborn, London WC1V 7QX

First published in the United States of America in 2022 by
Thames & Hudson Inc., 500 Fifth Avenue, New York, New York 10110

*Make Break Remix: The Rise of K-style* © 2022 Thames & Hudson Ltd, London

Text © 2022 Fiona Bae
Photographs unless otherwise stated © 2022 less_TAEKYUN KIM
Designed by Hezin O

British Library Cataloguing-in-Publication Data
A catalogue record for this book is available from the British Library

Library of Congress Control Number 2022931218

ISBN 978-0-500-02454-6

Printed and bound in China by Artron Art (Group) Co. Ltd

MIX
Paper from
responsible sources
FSC® C019910

Be the first to know about our new releases,
exclusive content and author events by visiting
**thamesandhudson.com**
**thamesandhudsonusa.com**
**thamesandhudson.com.au**